BRAIN GAIN

BROOKINGS FOCUS BOOKS

Brooking Focus Books feature concise, accessible, and timely
assessment of pressing policy issues of interest to a broad audience.
Each book includes recommendations for action on the issue discussed.

Also in this series:
Fast Forward: Ethics and Politics in the Age of Global Warming
by William Antholis and Strobe Talbott

A BROOKINGS FOCUS BOOK

BRAIN GAIN

RETHINKING U.S. IMMIGRATION POLICY

Darrell M. West

BROOKINGS INSTITUTION PRESS
Washington, D.C.

Copyright © 2010

THE BROOKINGS INSTITUTION

1775 Massachusetts Avenue, N.W., Washington, D.C. 20036
www.brookings.edu

Library of Congress Cataloging-in-Publication data is available

ISBN 978-0-8157-0482-9 (hardcover : alk. paper)

9 8 7 6 5 4 3 2 1

Printed on acid-free paper

Typeset in Sabon

Composition by Cynthia Stock
Silver Spring, Maryland

Printed by R. R. Donnelley
Harrisonburg, Virginia

To Karin Rosnizeck

First my immigration problem,

now my immigration joy

CONTENTS

PREFACE

WHEN I MARRIED IN 2007, I had no idea how complicated it would be to bring my wife, a German, to America and get her a work permit. She was well educated, spoke fluent English, and had a security clearance from her public affairs job at the U.S. State Department in Munich. I expected her entry would be easy because of the timeworn Statute of Liberty narrative about America valuing immigrant contributions. The United States emphasizes a tradition of welcoming new arrivals and appreciating their hard work and entrepreneurial spirit. This view has been reinforced during recent times by a national dialogue that has stressed globalization and the idea that countries should lower national boundaries to encourage global trade and commerce.

Confronted by the myriad problems of trying to gain entry for my bride, though, I discovered a more complicated reality underneath the Statue of Liberty story line. Immigration is controversial now and has been throughout much of American history. Even as the statue was dedicated in 1886, opposition was brewing to the millions of foreigners who migrated to the United States between 1860 and 1920. Critics wondered how these new people, with their different languages, cultures, and religions would alter the American character, and what social and economic problems might emerge.

Shortly before the dedication, Congress passed the Chinese Exclusion Act of 1882 that singled out Chinese for discriminatory treatment. The movement of individuals from Great Britain, Scotland, Ireland, France, Germany, the Netherlands, and Italy also sparked worry regarding immigration. In the twentieth century, political leaders imposed border controls, quotas, and overall caps on new arrivals. During the Great Depression, immigration ground almost completely to a halt as President Franklin Roosevelt and members of Congress fought to keep scarce U.S. jobs for existing residents.

The immigration story became even more challenging in the mid-twentieth century, when the ethnic character of immigration shifted. Rather than coming from European stock, the new immigrants entered from Asia, Africa, the Caribbean, Central America, and Mexico. They looked and sounded different from those already in the United States. Questions again arose regarding what it meant to be an American when the new arrivals had a native language other than English and were of a different racial or ethnic background. Critics worried that these individuals would not integrate, would alter the melting-pot character of the "American" culture, and would take desirable jobs from native-born Americans.

As the total annual number of lawful immigrants rose from 270,000 in 1980 to over 1 million today, a number of media and political leaders have taken a tough rhetorical stance on legal and (especially) illegal immigration. In 1986 the Immigration Reform and Control Act established penalties for businesses that knowingly hired illegal immigrants. The United States expanded categories for alien punishment and deportation in the 1996 Antiterrorism and Effective Death Penalty Act and the 1996 Illegal Immigration Reform and Immigrant Responsibility Act, and in administrative decisions following the September 11, 2001, terrorist attacks.

Over the past decade, more than 2 million undocumented aliens have been expelled from the United States.

By the early twenty-first century, when my wife wanted to migrate, the immigration process was costly, highly bureaucratic, filled with barriers, and slow moving. Even in the seemingly straightforward case of a well-educated spouse with a master's degree in American studies, I had to fill out numerous forms, pay thousands of dollars, certify that I could guarantee a good standard of living, submit past tax and income documents, have her sign away future rights to social welfare benefits, go through a personal interview to make sure we had a bona fide relationship, and have her pass medical certifications and biometrics inspections to guarantee she would not subject the United States to serious health or security risks. We overcame each barrier but only with considerable time, financial resources, and knowledge of American government. Even with a doctorate in political science, I found it difficult to figure out how to navigate this complex system.

Our immigration process has become tougher on new arrivals because many native-borns are anxious and angry. Conservatives fret that porous borders allow criminals, terrorists, and other illegal immigrants to enter the United States in dangerous numbers and that undocumented aliens unfairly receive social and financial benefits in housing, education, and public assistance. Progressives are no happier. They feel that government enforcement is overly harsh and selective, that policies divide families, and that immigration policy is filled with inequities. Businesses worry they are not getting the highly skilled workers they need. Higher education institutions are unhappy because of difficulties obtaining educational visas for foreign students. The inability of Congress to address these concerns has left a status quo that satisfies virtually no one.

THE RATIONALE FOR REFORM

This book addresses why immigration policy has become difficult to resolve politically despite evidence of substantial social, economic, intellectual, and cultural benefits for the United States. Some of the country's greatest artists, investors, entrepreneurs, and leaders have come from abroad. Advances in atomic energy, information technology, international commerce, sports, arts, and culture are directly attributable to talented immigrants. Indeed, I argue that America experiences a "brain gain" from in-migration and therefore needs to maintain its openness to new arrivals to stay competitive and gain access to the special talents of other lands.

My central argument is that U.S. immigration policy went seriously off course after Congress passed legislation in 1965 making family unification the overarching principle in immigration policy. By focusing so much on people's ability to bring aunts, uncles, and cousins, the country has lost opportunities to find the next Albert Einstein, Sergey Brin, Vartan Gregorian, or Andrew Grove. We need to reconceptualize immigration as a brain gain and competitiveness enhancer for the United States. In-migration is a way to bring new skills to the country and take advantage of the entrepreneurial spirit that exists all around the world.

Recent efforts at immigration reform have failed because they have done little to address obvious political and policy problems. One striking feature is that American policy is not very strategic at using people's interest in coming to America to advance the country's long-term national objectives. Unlike other nations such as Australia and Canada, the United States does little to encourage immigration for purposes of economic development. Only limited efforts are made to retain international students after they graduate from U.S. colleges and universities. Most of them return to their home countries without being given an opportunity to stay in America.

The seeming irrationality of immigration policy arises from a variety of political, public opinion, and media-related reasons. Competing policy principles are hard to reconcile. Particularistic politics and fragmented institutions undermine America's ability to make sound public policy. Discussions about immigration often are emotional, volatile, and full of fear and anxiety. Because the subject touches on delicate issues of family, jobs, education, social service delivery, culture, language, and national character, it is hard for elected officials to deliberate effectively. Polarized institutions, unfair media coverage, complex public opinion, and difficulties in the administrative implementation of border enforcement and legal justice all contribute to the problem.

What is needed are policy changes that encourage long-term economic development without introducing unfair class, racial, or ethnic biases. A "brain gain" policy does not mean admitting only educated, white people from Europe. There are talented Asians, Africans, and Hispanics around the world, and many from poor or working-class backgrounds. The entrepreneurial spirit that exists in many cultures should be harnessed to bring talented individuals to our shores.

OVERVIEW OF THE BOOK

This research relies on several different data sources: elite opinion, national public opinion surveys, analyses of media coverage, study of administrative actions on enforcement and legal justice, and a history of legislative actions. First, I draw on the perspectives of leaders in the area of immigration. Analyzing the views of representatives from Congress, the White House, and advocacy organizations, I seek to determine why past efforts at immigration reform have failed and what needs to happen in the future for reform to succeed.

Second, I present the results of an analysis regarding media coverage of immigration. I show how immigrants are unfairly portrayed and how some media portraits have complicated the task of legislative deliberation. In the most recent round of congressional consideration of this issue in 2006 and 2007, for example, cable television and radio talk show hosts undermined legislative decisionmaking by focusing on undeserving illegals and possible terrorists and by promoting the ethnocentric view that foreigners were dangerous to the United States. This narrative of "illegality" permeated news coverage and overwhelmed themes focused on immigrant contributions to American life.

Third, to see how citizens feel about immigration, I analyzed national public opinion surveys conducted over the past fifty years. These surveys asked detailed questions about public priorities, areas of possible consensus, concerns about immigration, appetite for comprehensive versus incremental reform, and views about reform measures as well as common political and demographic determinants (sex, age, race, income, education, and party identification). The responses to these surveys help explain why Americans hold the attitudes they do and how opinions have shifted at various points in time.

Fourth, I investigate administrative actions in the areas of legal justice and border enforcement. Using information from deportation proceedings, legal venues, and border enforcement, I discuss how toughened border enforcement has helped to stem the flow of illegal immigrants and why effective border security helps ease public anxiety over immigration.

Finally, a variety of documentary evidence about past and current legislative actions on immigration reform allows me to study how past stalemates developed and to suggest ways that they can be broken in the future. Although immigration features complex political, social, and economic dynamics, there are policy changes that would reassure the American public and facilitate the passage of comprehensive reform.

The outline of this book is as follows. In chapter 1, I examine the economic, intellectual, and social costs and benefits of immigration to the United States. I argue briefly that immigration has brought an impressive number of business and artistic visionaries to the United States. This chapter reviews the contributions of naturalized citizens to American commerce, education, science, technology, arts, and culture, and makes the argument that our immigration "brain gain" outweighs its cost.

Chapter 2 notes that immigration is complicated because of the competing principles we seek to maximize: equity, openness, economic growth, family integration, social justice, and border security. Policies that maximize all these objectives are hard to devise. Immigration needs to be reconceptualized as a policy trade-off among national goals we wish to achieve. While a variety of important principles lie in this area, investing in human capital and strengthening international competitiveness should be at the top of the list. Having family integration as the dominant principle weakens our ability to pursue other desired priorities and makes it impossible to have a balanced and strategic national immigration policy.

In chapter 3, I argue that the history of legislative action on immigration shows the limits of particularistic politics in complex policy areas. In examining the evolution of American immigration policy, it is clear that politics has driven policy in undesirable ways. We often have made shortsighted decisions (such as passing legislation to exclude Chinese in the nineteenth century) or overreacted to public opinion (such as the fear of people of Arabic heritage after 9/11). We need political deliberations that focus on long-term national objectives as well as institutional structures that insulate elected officials from impossible political choices (such as the current difficult trade-off between admitting more extended family members versus high-skilled foreign workers).

Chapter 4 demonstrates that some of the worst decisions on immigration policy have been inflamed by media coverage that portrayed immigrants as dirty, dangerous, and un-American. I review nineteenth-century newspaper coverage of Chinese immigrants who helped build our national railroads, the Irish and Italians who labored in late nineteenth- and early twentieth-century factories, and more recent portraits of Asian, African, and Latin American immigrants. Repeatedly, much of the news reporting and especially commentary have played to common stereotypes and unfavorable narratives about new arrivals, and this bias has made it difficult for residents to understand immigration and for public officials to make sound policy choices.

In chapter 5, I show how public opinion on immigration is complex and volatile. Anxiety and anger about immigration colors many citizens' view of immigration policy. Public attitudes shift with events that are in the news, and citizens often have demonstrated xenophobic qualities that compromise rational policymaking. While the country has experienced some periods of relative liberalization, many eras feature public attitudes that are anti-immigrant, prejudiced, and discriminatory. Emotional public opinion trends have colored public policy and compromised national deliberations on immigration.

Chapter 6 finds that immigration policy has been plagued by unequal justice, selective enforcement, and an inability to safeguard America's borders. Current legal proceedings feature defendants with no counsel advising them of rights and procedures, leading to inequities in court decisions on deportation. Laws penalizing businesses that rely on undocumented aliens are selectively enforced. Many companies are overlooked, while others are raided and prosecuted. Ineffectiveness in dealing with enforcement issues has made it difficult to generate much confidence both among the immigrant community and the American public at large.

In chapter 7, I suggest the way to overcome policy stalemate on this issue is to reconceptualize the immigration narrative as a brain gain for the United States. If the country wishes to benefit from future immigrant geniuses similar to the Einsteins of the past, illegal immigration will need to be reduced and legal immigration strengthened in a way that draws top international talent. Balancing the personal and humanitarian virtue of family integration with long-term national objectives such as improving competitiveness and attracting high-skilled workers is vital. We need to overcome particularistic politics and view immigration as a social, economic, and cultural benefit for the country.

I want to acknowledge the help of several individuals and organizations. Jenny Lu provided valuable research assistance on this project. Bill Galston and his colleagues on the Brookings Immigration Roundtable helped clarify key trade-offs in the immigration area. Nicholas Valentino and James Gimpel provided valuable reviews of the preliminary manuscript, and I am grateful for their very helpful comments. The Brookings Governance Studies program provided time and resources for this project. Marty Gottron did a superb job editing the manuscript. I appreciate the assistance of Brookings Institution Press officials Robert Faherty, Chris Kelaher, and Janet Walker in shepherding this manuscript through the publication process. None of these individuals or organizations is responsible for the interpretations presented here.

CHAPTER ONE

THE COSTS AND BENEFITS OF IMMIGRATION

FEW ISSUES ARE MORE CONTROVERSIAL than immigration.[1] The flood of illegal immigrants across U.S. borders enrages many native-born residents who believe that immigrants compete for jobs, unfairly draw on government benefits, and fundamentally alter the social fabric of America. These native-borns fear that non-English-speaking foreigners who move to the United States—legally or illegally—and do not integrate into mainstream social and political life are threatening to erase our culture's distinctive character.

Part of this anxiety is rooted in ethnocentrism and group animus. People tend not to like others who look or act differently from themselves. As Donald Kinder and Cindy Kam noted in their recent book, ethnocentrism is common in many different societies. People divide themselves into "in-groups and out-groups," and these types of "us versus them" distinctions color public opinion and make it difficult to develop balanced public policies.[2]

Others are concerned about immigration because they view the material costs of open-door policies as broad-based but see the benefits as concentrated. As researcher Gary Freeman argued, the impact of open policies falls on disadvantaged workers who feel their wages are depressed by newcomers and on taxpayers who worry about a drain on public resources, while the benefits accrue to small groups of successful immigrants who get good jobs and to some businesses that gain the skills of new arrivals.[3]

Both ideas (group animosity and unfavorable cost-benefit ratios) make it virtually impossible for the American political system to resolve the many conflicts involving immigration. Many taxpayers feel that immigrants receive more benefits than they deserve and that the social costs of undocumented arrivals are enormous. As long as these are the prevailing citizen interpretations, immigration will remain controversial, many will favor punitive policies, and political leaders will find it impossible to address this topic.[4]

In this book, I seek to reframe the public debate over immigration policy by arguing that the benefits of immigration are much broader than popularly imagined and the costs are more confined. Despite legitimate fear and anxiety over illegal immigration, I suggest that immigrants bring a "brain gain" of innovation and creativity that outweighs real or imagined costs. Throughout the nation's history, immigrants have enriched economic, intellectual, social, and cultural life in the United States in a number of fundamental respects.[5] The nation needs a new national narrative on immigration that moves from themes of illegality and abuse to innovation and enrichment. The country needs to build a new public policy based on empirical realities, not abstract fears and emotions.

To build a stronger case for immigration, the government needs to make policy changes that promote the benefits of immigration, while simultaneously adopting policies that reduce fears about its social and material costs. Policymakers should expand visa programs that bring talented and entrepreneurial foreigners to the country.[6] And the government should take border and employment security seriously to ease citizen concern about the impact of illegal immigrants on national life. These actions will not completely reassure those who oppose immigration based on group animosity or economic impact. But if these policy shifts are adopted, they will help citizens see the virtues of in-migration and make them less anxious about new arrivals.

A BRIEF HISTORY OF IMMIGRATION

From 1820 to 1920 nearly 30 million foreigners arrived in the United States. Close to 400,000 immigrants arrived in 1870 alone; ten years later that figure rose to over 450,000 and remained high for several years.[7] These migrants transformed America, supplying labor for the great industrialization that swept over the country. But their presence also ignited sharp divisions over the character and impact of foreign immigration. Indeed, many of the current debates mirror arguments that took place more than 100 years ago.

Over the course of the twentieth century, the level of American immigration has fluctuated considerably depending on political and economic circumstances.[8] As shown in figure 1-1, in-migration between 1860 and 2007 reached a high point of over 1.2 million individuals in 1907, but then dropped to under 300,000 in 1917 toward the end of World War I. Levels rose again during the 1920s but slowed to a trickle during the Great Depression of the 1930s. In the last few years, levels rose to around 1 million new entries each year. Today, around 13 percent of immigrants are first-generation arrivals, while 11 percent are American-born children of immigrants.[9]

Early immigrant waves in the eighteenth and nineteenth centuries came largely from European stock. These initial migrations gave us our language and people with experience in farming, business, and trade. The Germans arrived in the 1840s and 1850s, seeking land and fortune in the Midwestern part of the country. They were followed by Russians, Irish, and Italians in subsequent decades.[10] With this mix of ethnic backgrounds, the image of the "melting pot" became the prevailing metaphor of this time period.

In the mid-twentieth century, though, the main countries of origin shifted south and east. The largest sources of immigration

FIGURE 1-1. Number of Lawful Immigrants, 1820–2007

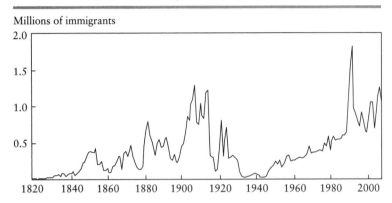

Source: U.S. Dept of Homeland Security, Office of Immigration Statistics, *Yearbook of Immigration Statistics*, 2007(www.dhs.gov/xlibrary/assets/statistics/yearbook/2007/table01.xls).

in recent years have been Asia, South and Central America, and Africa. Of the 1,052,415 legal permanent residents who came to America in 2007, 36 percent emigrated from Asia; 32 percent entered from the Caribbean, Central America, or other parts of North America; 11 percent migrated from Europe; 10 percent arrived from South America; and 9 percent came from Africa. The largest single country of origin was Mexico (14.1 percent of all lawful immigrants), followed by China (7.3 percent), the Philippines (6.9 percent), and India (6.2 percent).[11]

These immigrant waves were very controversial.[12] The languages, even the alphabets, of these new arrivals were unfamiliar, and the immigrants themselves were racially and ethnically different from their European predecessors. In many cases their religious, cultural, and political backgrounds differed significantly, and it was harder for them to assimilate.[13] Americans did not always accept them as fellow countrymen and women, and their cultural distinctiveness would put the idea of a melting pot to a fundamental test.

The large population movements over the past decades are not just a U.S. phenomenon. In 2008 there were an estimated 191 million "transnational immigrants" and over 30 million political refugees around the world.[14] With the advent of civil wars, natural disasters, economic inequality, and relatively cheap air travel, migration has become a growth industry. Indeed, the economies of many developing countries rely heavily on the remittances migrants send home to their families from their earnings abroad. People move not only to gain better economic conditions, but to reunite with families, seek freedom of political expression, or escape poor personal circumstances.[15]

With large numbers of people on the move, widespread migration has become one of the defining hallmarks of the contemporary period. The previous era, when individuals tended to stay close to home, is over. People's vision of the world has broadened with the advent of global media such as television and the Internet. Those thinking about going elsewhere can see what the alternatives are and appear to have fewer inhibitions about resettling, especially when conditions in their home country are not very favorable for economic or political reasons.

Immigration is a serious political issue in many countries besides the United States. Comparisons of attitudes toward immigration in western nations shows the United States to be about at the midpoint in the share of residents who think immigration is a problem. According to national surveys, the western country with the highest percentage of citizens who feel immigration is a problem is the United Kingdom (62 percent), followed by 50 percent in the United States, 49 percent in Germany, 47 percent in Italy, 41 percent in Poland, 38 percent in the Netherlands, and 35 percent in France.[16] The variation in public attitudes across these nations suggests that citizen anxiety can be managed even when foreigners look and act differently from native-borns. What is needed are national policies that understand the source of public discontent and take actions to minimize public perceptions of immigrant social and economic costs.

IMMIGRATION PATHWAYS

Immigrants come to the United States in three general ways. First, they can become legal permanent residents through marriage, extended family ties, or special skills, or as political refugees. Using visas known as green cards, legal permanent residents are able to live and work in the country. Of the 35 million American immigrants in the United States, an estimated two-thirds (around 23 million) are legal permanent residents.[17] Individuals with green cards can apply for U.S. citizenship after five years and become naturalized citizens with full rights such as voting and eligibility for social service benefits.

The second route is through temporary work or tourism visas or through short-term visas for student or government exchanges. These are individuals who come to America for limited periods of time to visit, work, attend government or academic events, or enroll in educational institutions. Among the nation's immigrants, only about 3 percent (or 1 million people) enter the United States through one of these avenues. Of them, 65,000 arrive through the H-1B visa program for high-skilled workers and 66,000 come through the H-2A or H-2B program for seasonal workers in agriculture, construction, or tourism.[18] They are allowed to work in America for three years.

The high-skilled visa program was expanded to 115,000 in 1999 and to 195,000 in 2001 but dropped back to 65,000 in 2004 when Congress did not renew the temporary increases. Critics complained that this entry program disadvantaged American workers and kept wages down for American scientists.[19] In 2009, when the country was enduring a deep recession, Congress voted to restrict financial firms' use of the H-1B visa program. Those financial firms that receiving federal bailout money had to try to hire American workers and then document there were no qualified American applicants before employing foreign-borns.[20] The Obama administration has pledged tighter oversight of this program to make sure native-born workers receive fair consideration from companies hiring new, high-skilled employees.[21]

The third and most controversial mechanism is illegal immigration. It is estimated that one-third of all immigrants (or 11.9 million individuals) are in the United States illegally, many from Mexico. These overall numbers are up from 5 million in 1996 and 8.4 million in 2000. The U.S. Border Patrol reports that 97 percent of illegal border crossers enter the United States through Mexico.[22] According to statistics compiled by the Border Patrol, the number of individuals arrested for attempting to sneak over the Mexican line has fluctuated over the past thirty years. The number arrested was 1.7 million in the mid-1980s, 1 million in the late 1980s, 1.6 million in 2000, and 705,000 in 2008. The latter was the lowest number of border-crossing arrests since 675,000 were stopped in 1976. Beefed-up security and a bad economy apparently discouraged some in-migration. Since 2006, 6,000 border patrol agents have been added along the Mexican boundary and 526 miles of fence have been built to enhance enforcement.[23]

Historically, legal and illegal immigrants have clustered in border states, river ports, or coastal communities, places that were accessible to new arrivals. The East and West Coasts, along with areas bordering Mexico, attracted the most immigrants. Cities such as New York, Los Angeles, San Francisco, Seattle, Boston, Philadelphia, and Chicago had sizable immigrant populations, as did most southwestern states.

In recent years, though, new immigrant gateway communities have arisen. Immigration has spread from the traditional cities to venues such as Dallas, Las Vegas, Charlotte, Phoenix, Denver, Minneapolis, and Atlanta. In addition, immigration no longer is an urban story but has spread to suburban areas. As Brookings Institution scholar Audrey Singer has noted, many of these areas were populated predominantly by the native-born in 1970 but now have fast-growing immigrant populations.[24]

This transformation affects the politics, economy, and social integration of immigration. The push into areas where few immigrants previously lived sometimes disturbs local residents and provokes a public opinion backlash. People who live in homogeneous areas and are not used to people of different backgrounds may have difficulty adjusting to the new demographic mix. They may worry about a drain on public resources and other real or perceived fiscal impacts arising from immigration.

These attitudes complicate political consideration of immigration reform and the ability of lawmakers to forge public policy. Conflict between old and new populations can be sharp. Unless arrivals are integrated into the community, local communities can have trouble reconciling the resulting social and political conflict. Some cities in this situation have moved toward inclusive policies, while others have pushed for restrictive efforts. Whether new arrivals are refugees, what their country of origin is, and how these immigrants affect crime, housing, and local economies all affect how native-borns feel about them.[25]

Some studies have found that the recent recession has slowed the immigrant flow. Not only are fewer immigrants coming to America, but many already in the United States are returning to their original countries. With some developing countries enjoying a strong economy as the United States struggles with a weak one, immigrants appear to see fewer reasons to come to America than previously was the case.[26] Whether this development is a long- or short-term one is unknown, but it represents an interesting divergence from earlier periods of prosperity.

ECONOMIC COSTS AND BENEFITS

A number of attempts have been made to estimate immigration's economic costs and benefits to the United States.[27] Some of the analysis is based on perceptual research that relies on public opinion polls showing people's impressions of costs versus benefits. For example, when respondents were asked specifically about jobs created and lost because of immigration, one poll found that 51 percent of those surveyed said they believe that immigrants take jobs away from native-born workers. However, 86 percent believe that immigrants are hard workers, and 61 percent think immigrants create jobs and set up new businesses.[28]

More reliable studies use employment, wage, and other types of economic data designed to measure the objective reality. These projects look at the ramifications of immigration for use of government services, tax payments, health care utilization, Social Security contributions, labor force participation, wage levels, and gross domestic product (GDP).

Not surprising, given the complexity of these calculations, the net impact of in-migration is difficult to isolate.[29] The results of these studies vary greatly depending on whether the unit analyzed is the individual, family, or extended family. Immigrants represent one-tenth of the overall American population, so the tremendous variety of ages, life situations, and economic circumstances makes modeling their impact challenging.

What one concludes about the exact fiscal impact also shifts tremendously with assumptions regarding tax, health, education, and pension utilization. Typically, younger immigrants with school-age children or older immigrants who draw on health care and pensions cost the most, while young people with no children and middle-aged households with children past education age but with members who do not yet require considerable health or pension services cost the least (as is the case with native-born Americans). To determine the actual costs and benefits of immigration, then, one needs to know the age, family status, number of children, health requirements, education needs, and pension situation for the individuals in question plus the contributions the individuals have made in tax, Social Security, and Medicare payments.

Research has found that new immigrants tend to come to America as young workers, when they are paying taxes and not drawing extensively on public pensions or health care. For example, 24.6 percent of adult immigrants are aged 25 to 34 and 28.3 percent are 35 to 44 years old. Only 4.4 percent are 65 years or older.[30] From a collective standpoint, the virtue of this distribution is that it enhances the economic benefits of immigration.[31] Young immigrants are more likely to be taxpayers than to require public services. They also are more likely to become homeowners and to pay property taxes.[32] But the older the immigration pool, the more likely individuals are to be beyond their prime working years and to require expensive government health and pension benefits.

Most immigrants, legal or illegal, are not allowed to participate in Medicaid, Supplemental Security Income, food stamps, Temporary Assistance to Needy Families, or the State Children's Health Insurance program. Illegal immigrants are not able to receive any forms of welfare, public health care (except for emergency services), or retirement benefits. Legal permanent residents must contribute to Medicare and Social Security for at least ten years before they can benefit from these government programs.

If born in the United States, though, children of immigrants are American citizens and can receive government aid targeted on the young. Research shows that three-quarters of the children of illegal immigrants—around 4 million children—were born in the United States and therefore are considered legal residents.[33] A new provision of the State Children's Health Insurance Program enacted in 2009 allows children of legal immigrants to receive health coverage immediately, as opposed to waiting five years, as previously had been the case.[34]

Fiscal pressures, though, have led some state governments to eliminate health coverage for legal immigrants as a way to close budget gaps. For example, Massachusetts had some of the most generous health coverage provisions for immigrants in the nation, yet its fiscal 2010 budget dropped insurance for 30,000 legal immigrants who had held a green card for fewer than five years. Public authorities justified this move mainly on fiscal grounds.[35]

Of course, despite particular rules, some immigrants receive public assistance. However, studies have found that the percentage receiving aid is smaller than for U.S. households as a whole. Overall, 5 percent of American households receive cash assistance, compared to 1 percent for undocumented immigrants who obtain benefits using false documents.[36]

The exception to this general pattern for public service delivery occurs with education. Under a 1982 U.S. Supreme Court decision, *Plyler v. Doe,* states and localities cannot deny immigrants access to elementary or secondary education. The case involved a 1975 Texas law that withheld education funding for children who came to the country illegally and that allowed local schools to deny enrollment to these pupils. On a 5 to 4 vote, the Supreme Court ruled that this law violated the Fourteenth Amendment and therefore was unconstitutional. Schools must educate children whether they are legal or illegal residents of the United States.

The same logic applies to emergency health care. On the principle than everyone deserves care, hospital emergency rooms are supposed to treat patients no matter their legal status or their ability to pay. In reality, however, undocumented individuals tend to get less care than citizens or legal immigrants. One California study found that "undocumented Mexicans and other undocumented Latinos reported less use of health care services and poorer experiences with care compared with their U.S.-born counterparts."[37]

Labor force participation and tax payments represent another area of impact. Several studies have found that immigrants pay income, Social Security, and Medicare taxes. A National Immigration Forum and Cato Institute report estimated that immigrants paid $162 billion annually in federal, state, and local taxes.[38] A study by the National Research Council concluded that "the average immigrant pays nearly $1,800 more in taxes than he or she costs in benefits."[39] One of the myths about illegal immigrants is that they pay no taxes. In fact, many pay taxes even when they are ineligible to collect social service benefits. Undocumented aliens pay sales taxes on purchases they make in the same way any consumer would. If they own or rent housing, they pay property taxes related to the accommodations. And it has been estimated that "between one-half and three-quarters of undocumented immigrants pay federal and state income taxes."[40]

Hardest to estimate is immigrants' contribution to GDP—the total value of all goods and services produced in the United States. Modeling overall economic contributions is challenging because of the complexity of the subject. But a 2007 study by the White House Council of Economic Advisors concluded that immigrants raised American GDP by $37 billion a year.[41] It has been estimated that immigration adds one-third of total population growth in the United States.[42] Because they buy food, pay for housing, enjoy entertainment, get hair cuts, and spend money on a range of commercial services, there is little doubt immigrants generate considerable economic activity.

During recessions, the greatest fear about immigration (legal or illegal) is the "crowding-out" effect. Critics fear that foreigners take jobs that otherwise would go to Americans or reduce wage gains through increased job competition. Some evidence indicates that immigrants do have negative wage effects for those native-born Americans without a high school diploma. For these individuals, immigration caused a 1.1 percent drop in yearly wages.[43] The same study found, however, that for most other workers, immigrants complement, rather than substitute for, the efforts of American workers. Researchers found that "90 percent of native-born workers with at least a high-school diploma experienced wage gains from immigration ranging from 0.7 percent to 3.4 percent, depending on education."[44] For those people, the crowding-out effect is not a major problem.

Another project, conducted during the recent recession, found no difference in the jobless rates of foreign and native-born workers. But while each had the same unemployment level, the type of work performed differed. According to the U.S. Bureau of Labor Statistics, foreign-born workers were more likely than other workers to find jobs in the service industry, transportation, or material-moving occupations.[45] They often take entry-level jobs in custodial services, restaurants, or construction that are poorly paid and not very desirable.[46]

For completely understandable reasons, people grow more fearful about immigration during periods of rising unemployment. Analysis undertaken by Brookings Institution researcher E. J. Dionne demonstrates the intertwining of economic conditions with public opinion regarding immigration. Over the past decade, views about the desirable number of immigrants correlated highly with the national unemployment rate. When unemployment rose, Dionne found, more Americans thought immigration should be cut back, and when it dropped, fewer felt that way.[47]

As a long-term matter, policymakers need to pay attention to U.S. competitiveness and the contributions immigrants make to the economy. Immigrants spend money on goods and services, pay taxes, and perform jobs many American citizens view as undesirable. They also have made significant contributions to American science and economic enterprise, particularly in the areas of high-tech and biotech. Recent clampdowns on the number who can stay aggravate our international competitiveness situation. Universities invest millions in training foreign students and often provide free tuition to Ph.D. students, but upon graduation, many of them are not given any U.S. job opportunities that would take advantage of their new skills and instead return home. This practice robs the United States of the ability to reap the benefits of its economic investment in higher education.

HIGH-TECH DEVELOPMENT

Several studies have documented the scientific and economic contributions skilled immigrants have made to the high-tech and biotech industries. According to one study, 25.3 percent of the technology and engineering businesses launched in the United States between 1995 to 2005 had a foreign-born founder. In California this percentage was 38.8 percent. And in Silicon Valley, the center of the high-tech industry, 52.4 percent of the new tech start-ups had a foreign-born owner. According to the study's count, "Immigrant-founded companies produced $52 billion in sales and employed 450,000 workers in 2005."[48]

The same report found that nearly a quarter (24.2 percent) of the international patents filed from the United States in 2006 were based on the work of foreign-borns living in America, an increase from 7.3 percent in 1998.[49] Consistent with a brain-gain hypothesis, many of these patent-holders held degrees in science, technology, engineering, or math and were educated at American universities. Fifty-three percent of them received their highest degree from a U.S. university, suggesting that there is great value in bringing the foreign-born to America, educating them, and keeping them here in U.S. jobs.[50]

Scholars Gnanaraj Chellaraj, Keith Maskus, and Aaditya Mattoo have estimated the impact of immigration on patent applications and awards and found that international graduate students and skilled immigrants have a positive impact on U.S. patent generation. Their figures demonstrate that increasing "the number of foreign graduate students would raise patent applications by 4.7 percent, university patent grants by 5.3 percent and non-university patent grants by 6.7 percent."[51]

Indeed, most founders of high-tech companies who came to America from abroad did so as students and then started business careers after graduation. Many foreign students are highly motivated individuals who would like to stay in the United States after graduation to work, launch businesses, and develop innovative ideas. They are a source of great talent and an engine for economic development.

According to the Kauffman Index of Entrepreneurial Activity, immigrants over the past decade have displayed a high level of entrepreneurial spirit. Between 1996 and 2008, immigrants were twice as likely as native-borns to start new businesses. In 2008, for example, more than 5 percent of immigrants launched a business, compared with fewer than 3 percent of native-born individuals.[52]

Social scientist AnnaLee Saxenian traces the rise of America's high-tech boom to congressional passage of the Immigration Act of 1965 (also known as the Hart-Celler Act). As far back as the Johnson-Reid Immigration Act of 1924, the United States imposed strict limits on immigration from specific countries. For example, Taiwan and many other Asian nations were each limited to 100 immigrants a year, which placed a tight cap on Asian scientists and engineers. The Hart-Celler Act raised those caps exponentially, starting Asia's brain drain by creating opportunities for foreigners with special skills to migrate to America. Later legislation such as the Immigration and Nationality Act of 1990 expanded these opportunities by boosting visas based on technical talent.[53]

According to Saxenian, it is no coincidence that the high-tech boom began when Asian scientists and engineers began to come to the United States in large numbers. Silicon Valley started to attract Chinese and Indian talent immediately after 1965. Based on her research, there were 92,020 Chinese and 28,520 Indians in the Silicon Valley workforce by 1990, and "84 percent of the Chinese and 98 percent of the Indians were immigrants."[54] These numbers grew even larger in the 1990s and early 2000s.

The number of foreign students admitted to American science and engineering graduate programs also rose during this period. With the help of federal financial aid programs and increases in research and development funding, American universities grew substantially and expanded the size of their Ph.D. programs. From 1960 to 2000 the raw number of international students increased eightfold. The share of U.S. doctorates held by foreign-born students rose from 23 percent in 1966 to 39 percent in 2000.[55]

But this trend slowed after the September 11, 2001, terrorist attacks in New York City and Washington, D.C., and the resulting changes in foreign student visa rules. The U.S. government made it more difficult for foreigners to obtain student visas and enroll in American universities. This slowdown in higher education is worrisome because a recent national survey found that more than two-thirds of Americans said they thought immigrants improved U.S. culture with new ideas.[56] This finding provides perceptual support for the argument that immigrants add value, diversity, and ideas to civic life. So too do several examples of individual immigrants who have made substantial contributions to American economic and cultural life.

One of these individuals is Sergey Brin, the founder of the pathbreaking search engine firm, Google. Born in Moscow, he moved to the United States at the age of six. His parents were mathematicians, and he quickly developed an aptitude for math and computer science. At Stanford University, he met classmate Larry Page, and the two combined their respective interests in data mining and search efficiency to form the now legendary and highly successful company.[57]

Google revolutionized computing by developing a very efficient Internet search engine. As the web grew in size and complexity, having good search features became essential to maximizing information usage. Search represented a way for people to tame the information flow and find the material they needed. It put people in charge of information, as opposed to the other way around. This innovation allowed the Internet to thrive and develop, as people turned to it for business, education, health care, and a myriad of other information needs.

Pierre Omidyar displayed a similar ingenuity. Born in Paris in 1967 of Iranian parents, he came to America as a young child. He earned a degree in computer science from Tufts University and served as a software developer for several computer companies. After working on an Internet shopping site, he designed an online auction service in 1995 that he called Auction Web. On this site, people could request bids for collectibles, and items were sold to the highest bidder. Two years later, he renamed the company eBay and soon had over 1 million customers. By 2003 the business had grown to 95 million registered users, had sales of over $2 billion, and was expanding into India and China.[58] Consistent with the digital era, he empowered ordinary folks and cut out the middle-man in business transactions, transforming commerce by directly connecting buyers and sellers and allowing markets in niche areas to flourish. His leadership paved the way for other Internet companies to thrive in various niches.

Andy Grove is a leader in the areas of semiconductors and microchips. Born in Budapest, Grove migrated to the United States, where he founded the Intel Corporation in 1968 and made it the leading company in the field. As microchips were made smaller and smaller, computers became cheaper and more powerful. The computing era would not have thrived to the extent it did without his leadership.[59]

Jerry Wang represents another example of an immigrant visionary. Born in Taiwan, he came to America when he was ten years old. In college his hobby was compiling links of favorite websites into a central service. This later formed the nucleus of his company, Yahoo. The firm eventually became a successful portal that offered news, entertainment, search, email, and social networking. It is estimated that nearly 500 million people around the world use his company's email service.[60]

SOCIAL COSTS AND BENEFITS

As challenging as is the computation of immigration's economic and intellectual contributions, the social costs and benefits are even harder to measure. Because they involve less tangible ramifications than taxes, employment, government benefits, or patents, the actual magnitude of social contributions is more challenging to estimate. People intuitively understand the social value that immigrants offer—in food, arts, culture, and athletics, among other things—but the value of these contributions is difficult to determine precisely.[61]

Researchers Gianmarco Ottaviano and Giovanni Peri attempt to evaluate the value of cultural diversity in the United States. They ask who can deny the value of "Italian restaurants, French beauty shops, German breweries, Belgian chocolate stores, Russian ballets, Chinese markets, and Indian tea houses." Through the globalization of food, culture, and artistic expression, metropolitan areas with greater diversity show higher wages. According to Ottaviano and Peri, American workers benefit because "a more multicultural urban environment makes U.S.-born citizens more productive."[62]

Richard Florida takes this argument one step further by suggesting a correlation between geographic diversity, innovation, and productivity. Cities that have diverse and creative residents tend to be more pleasant and productive places in which to live, in turn increasing innovation, home prices, the local economy, and civic pride, he argues.[63]

A 2007 Gallup Poll sought to get a handle on this subject by asking how immigrants had affected "food, music, and the arts" in America. Forty percent of the respondents indicated that immigrants had made things better, 9 percent felt they had made things worse, and 46 percent concluded there had not been much of an effect. Not surprisingly, there were substantial differences by race and ethnicity. Sixty-five percent of Hispanics felt immigrants had improved food, music, and the arts, compared with 34 percent of African-Americans, and 37 percent of whites.[64]

The internationalization of arts and culture has led to an influx of talented directors and performers from abroad. Of the seventeen Hollywood directors who have received multiple Academy Awards, nine were foreign born.[65] Individuals such as Salma Hayek, Mikhail Baryshnikov, Jim Carrey, and Dan Aykroyd are just a few examples of immigrants to the United States who have enriched the world of television, dancing, and film. Hayek is a Mexican-born actress who came to America for boarding school when she was twelve. She went on to leading roles in movies such as *Frida, Mi Vida Loca,* and *Wild Wild West.*

Baryshnikov is the world-renowned ballet dancer who was born in Riga, Latvia. In 1976 he defected from the Soviet Union to the United States and performed at the American Ballet Theatre, the New York City Ballet, and elsewhere around the world. Carrey is a comic actor born in Canada who has appeared in a variety of films such as *Ace Ventura, The Truman Show, The Cable Guy, The Mask,* and *Dumb and Dumber.* Aykroyd was a comedian and actor who also came to America from Canada. He starred on the television show *Saturday Night Live* and in films such as *Ghostbusters, Blues Brothers,* and *50 First Dates.*

The same argument holds for sports. It is hard to imagine contemporary American baseball without immigration. Baseball is a sport that used to be played by white Americans, then was integrated with African-Americans and American Hispanics, and now is populated by athletes from Japan, the Dominican Republic, Cuba, Jamaica, and Venezuela. In recent years, 29 percent of the players in Major League Baseball have been born outside the United States, mainly the Dominican Republic or Venezuela. One such star is Sammy Sosa, a leading home-run hitter from the Dominican Republic.[66]

Education and philanthropy also have benefited from the contributions of immigrants. One example is Vartan Gregorian, who was born in Tabriz, Iran, of Armenian heritage. Educated in Lebanon, he moved to America in 1956, where he eventually served as provost at the University of Pennsylvania, president of the New York Public Library, president of Brown University, and president of the Carnegie Corporation of New York, one of the leading philanthropic foundations in America. As a leading educator, author, and professor, he brought a strong sense of innovation to higher education and the world of philanthropy, showing leading institutions how to improve the plight of the disadvantaged and others passing through their doors.[67]

A number of political leaders have came from abroad to gain major elective or appointive positions in the United States. These include Governor Arnold Schwarzenegger of California, Governor Jennifer Granholm of Michigan, and former Secretary of State Madeleine Albright. Schwarzenegger is one of the most famous immigrant politicians. He arrived in the United States from Austria speaking no English. Following a career in body-building and Hollywood action films, Schwarzenegger was elected governor in 2003. Granholm, born in Vancouver, was educated at the University of California at Berkeley and Harvard Law School; she was elected governor in 2006. Albright was born in Prague and migrated to the United States. During the Clinton administration, she became U.S. Ambassador to the United Nations and then the first female secretary of state.[68]

CONCLUSION

In the end, the central question for immigration policy is the balance between costs and benefits. Vivek Wadhwa and colleagues reach a clear conclusion based on their studies. They say that "immigrants have become a significant driving force in the creation of new businesses and intellectual property in the U.S.—and that their contributions have increased over the past decade."[69]

In contrast to critics who worry that immigrants take American jobs and depress American wages, considerable research suggests that immigrants contribute to the vibrancy of American economic development and the richness of its cultural life. They start new businesses, patent novel ideas, and create jobs.

When one strips away the emotion and looks at the facts, the benefits of new arrivals to American innovation and entrepreneurship are abundant and easy to see. The costs immigrants impose are not zero, but those side-effects pale in comparison to the contributions arising from the immigrant brain gain.

CHAPTER TWO

COMPETING POLICY PRINCIPLES

IMMIGRATION IS A COMPLICATED POLICY issue because of the competing principles the United States seeks to maximize: international competitiveness, economic growth, innovation, family integration, social justice, and border security, among other things. From standpoints of both financial resources and political priorities, it is hard to devise policies that maximize all of these objectives.

Budgetwise, if the government spends billions constructing a fence along the Mexican border, authorities will not have adequate resources to promote faster administrative processing of visa applications or to provide legal counsel to immigrants facing deportation hearings. Politically, it is difficult to build coalitions that maximize all these goals because different groups value different principles. For example, many business and high-tech firms want more visas for workers with high-tech skills to help promote economic growth and innovation, while agricultural interests believe the need for low-cost, seasonal workers is crucial. Other groups say border security is the greatest priority because if U.S. entry points do not protect Americans from possible criminals or terrorists, it matters little what procedures are in place for prioritizing visa requests or promoting economic growth.

Historically, U.S. policy has emphasized very different approaches at various points in time. Early America was expanding geographically, so it valued the population growth and entrepreneurial activity provided by new arrivals. Given the preeminence of those goals, national policy generally emphasized open borders with minimal barriers to entry. There were some exceptions. For example, the Articles of Confederation restricted border entry by "paupers, vagabonds, and fugitives." But most who landed in the United States in the late 1700s and early 1800s were allowed to stay as long as they had good health and decent character.[1] And even the latter requirements were not rigorously enforced nationally at many points in time, although some states, especially in the South, did impose their own restrictions.[2]

As the foreign flows increased in the late 1800s and early 1900s, grassroots pressure for immigration restrictions intensified. Many Americans no longer supported an open policy for foreigners. Instead formal quotas were set for arrivals from each nation, and official checkpoints and entry requirements welcomed those wishing to migrate to America. Immigrants could not just show up and expect entry, as had been the case earlier in American history. Now they had to go through an elaborate, bureaucratic process that limited their ease of entry into the United States.

Newly released historical documents reveal how detailed this review process was. As part of a general effort to open up immigration records dating back to the 1800s, government immigration authorities have released official records of interviews, interrogations, and letters for specific individuals. One person named Thelma Lai Chang received a 103-page file of her father's efforts to enter the United States as a twelve-year-old boy in 1922. Many Chinese were barred from entry by the Chinese Exclusion Act, but Chang's father claimed he was the son of a family already living in America and was eventually admitted after being subjected to a detailed interrogation about his family history and background.[3]

In 1965 the United States enacted still another immigration regime that had a fundamentally different character than either of the earlier periods. For social and humanitarian reasons, policymakers during this national debate placed family integration at the center of national immigration policy. Lawmakers at the time believed that social considerations were more important than economic or security principles. In this comprehensive remaking of American immigration policy, the thought was that that family reunification in America was worthwhile because strong families were stable and productive. Research suggested that integrated families resulted in fewer social problems and led to higher educational attainment and better incomes.[4] The Hart-Celler Act of 1965 codified this social principle into law, and family integration become the prevailing goal for U.S. immigration policy.

Four decades later, this focus remains the most important objective in national decisionmaking. Today nearly two-thirds of the visas issued annually are distributed to individuals based on family ties. Unifying families spread out around the world is the paramount national policy goal for immigration.

The problem with this approach is that it slights competing priorities that are vital to the long-term future of the country. The current law does not take border security or crime perpetrated by illegal immigrants seriously enough for the general public, nor does it address America's very real economic needs for low-skilled agricultural workers, skilled engineers and scientists, and highly educated science and technology graduates of American universities whose tuition and learning are subsidized by the United States.[5]

Family is defined so broadly that eligibility includes not just immediate family members, for whom the benefits of unification are well documented, but the extended clan—aunts, uncles, cousins, adult children. Most research on the value of family integration is based on having mothers and fathers directly engaged in the rearing of children. It does not address the role of aunts, uncles, and cousins in family life. Indeed, little research supports the social or economic value of extended families on the upbringing of children. Extended relatives no doubt bring some value to child-rearing, such as additional income, but it is not clear that aunts or uncles play the same decisive role as parents.

I argue in this chapter that policymakers need to reconceptualize immigration as a policy trade-off and think systematically about desired national goals. While a variety of principles and objectives are important in this area, investing in human capital and strengthening international competitiveness deserve a higher priority. Right now America places very little value on attracting high- or low-skilled workers to its shores. Having family integration at the center of the current immigration agenda ignores other desired priorities and creates a status quo that does not generate adequate political support or serve long-term national economic interests.

EARLY POLICY: FOCUS ON MOSTLY OPEN BORDERS

Most American borders were open during the country's early history. The U.S. Articles of Confederation gave state and local governments the power to regulate their borders. Impoverished immigrants could be evicted if they were not legally settled in the community. Paupers and fugitives from the law were not welcome in many places.[6] Some worried about the assimilation of foreigners during these times. George Washington explained to foreign audiences that America wanted immigrants "who are determined to be sober, industrious and virtuous members of Society."[7]

Although immigration restrictions were not explicitly included in the Constitution, states guarded their prerogative over geographic borders. Southern states in particular had open borders for most settlers but restricted entry by blacks who had won their freedom.[8]

National policy had the explicit objective of welcoming newcomers and populating a vast continent. There was little government bureaucracy to review those who wanted to come to the

United States. The common mantra of this era was "Go West" to expand the reach of the young nation to the furthest western geographic part of the United States and to solidify U.S. claims against native Americans and foreign governments.

At the beginning of the nineteenth century, the United States consisted of the original thirteen colonies plus Vermont, Kentucky, and Tennessee in the Northeast, mid-Atlantic, and Southeast. By 1912 the nation had crossed the Mississippi River and expanded to the Pacific Ocean; forty-eight states covered all of the current continental United States.

A variety of explicit policy decisions contributed to this national expansion. Congress enacted generous homestead legislation designed to encourage people to move west. For example, the 1862 Homestead Act provided up to 640 acres to individuals willing to settle undeveloped areas outside the original thirteen colonies. Around 1.6 million homesteads totaling 270 million acres were granted to those wishing to resettle. The area they developed covered about 10 percent of all the American land that was part of the United States.[9]

The national government also encouraged expansion through the Morrill Land Grant Act of 1862. This legislation provided land to establish agricultural colleges that would teach subjects such as engineering, agriculture, and military strategy. By providing these kinds of educational opportunities at an inexpensive price, political authorities encouraged a large number of newcomers to come to America and settle its midwestern and western territories. They took advantage of the cheap educational institutions to develop their agricultural and scientific aptitudes.

Immigration was a vital part of America's national expansion strategy. National leaders realized the country could not grow fast enough through residential childbirth and that immigration represented a major key to U.S. expansion into the Midwest, Plains states, Southwest, and Far West. The country's economic development required a labor force that was willing and able to farm, ranch, and work in mines and factories. The work was hard and dangerous, the compensation not overly generous. Encouraging Europeans and others to migrate and settle not only represented a way to populate the new territories with hard-working entrepreneurial talent but was seen as vital to long-term economic development.[10]

For most immigrants during this period, the route to America was relatively simple. With a few exceptions, such as those pertaining to freed blacks in the South, new arrivals could travel and live wherever they wanted. There were limitations on becoming naturalized citizens, but virtually no restrictions on people who wanted to live in America without becoming formal citizens.

The country did not have much in the way of official immigrant screening until 1892, when Ellis Island and other processing centers were set up. Although mythologized as the quintessential symbol of American receptivity to new arrivals, the construction of Ellis Island actually reflected growing concerns about the risks of immigration. Near the end of the 1800s, native Americans were starting to worry about the flood of immigrants, many of whom did not speak English and came from places having very different cultures or backgrounds from those already here. Some citizens feared that these new arrivals would bring diseases and otherwise taint the character of American culture.

These concerns led to the establishment of new arrival processing centers on the East Coast. These facilities identified and screened immigrants for health status and other characteristics. Those with infectious diseases could be quarantined for a period of time. The Immigration Act of 1875 barred "prostitutes and criminals" from staying in the United States.[11] As of 1882 "lunatics" and people with serious diseases could be banned from entry. And in 1901, following the assassination of President William McKinley by an immigrant's son, foreign-born anarchists were banned.

As John Higham observed in his pathbreaking book *Strangers in the Land,* concerns about race, religion, and radical politics began to surface.[12] Restrictionists worried about political radicalism and the large number of Catholic immigrants entering the country, arguing that these new arrivals would bring "foreign" ideas to the United States and alter the existing national character.

For the first time in its young history, America was edging toward a serious reassessment of its national immigration policy. Rather than welcoming all newcomers, the United States was starting to single out particular groups for restrictive treatment. One ethnic group in particular, the Chinese, was treated particularly harshly and singled out for exclusionary treatment. Following waves of Chinese immigration between 1850 and 1870 to work on building railroads and other infrastructure projects, more and more citizens complained that the Chinese were distinctive and un-American, smoked opium, and did not assimilate to local culture.

Finally, national legislators enacted the Chinese Exclusion Act in 1882.[13] It limited new arrivals from China to a stay of no more than ten years. Workers who already were in the United States could stay as long as they had work visas and certificates of residency. Ten years later Congress bowed to continued public fear and resentment of Chinese immigrants and placed restrictions on Chinese immigrants already in America. The Geary Act of 1892 denied bail to Chinese accused of wrongdoing and required suspects to have an official "certificate of residency" and proof from a "white witness" that they had lived in the United States since 1882.[14] Those who were unable to provide proper documentation were deported.

These policy restrictions placed on Chinese in America were a harbinger of a brewing crackdown. Soon other nationalities would find that fears about jobs, health, national security, and the American character would trump the open border policy. Over the course of a few decades, a tidal wave of national resentment would lead to a dramatic reconfiguration of U.S. immigration policy, one that now restricted entry to the United States. [15]

EARLY 1900S: EMPHASIS ON IMMIGRATION RESTRICTIONS

By the 1920s public concern over unchecked immigration had reached new heights. In response Congress enacted the Emergency Quota Act of 1921, which established official quotas for immigrants based on national origins. Each nation was assigned a certain number of entry visas based on the number of its people living in the United States at the time of the 1910 census.

These quotas were codified and made permanent in 1924 by the Johnson-Reid Immigration Act. An overall ceiling of 154,227 arrivals from the Eastern Hemisphere was established, and each country given a specific number of new immigrants.[16] Because of continuing citizen anxiety over the number of new arrivals from southern and eastern Europe over the preceding decades, these limitations for all countries were set as of the 1890 census when fewer southern and eastern Europeans were present in the United States.

The legislation clearly marked a new era in American immigration history. No longer would the "open door" be the guiding principle of national policy. Instead, the country would set a low overall limit on immigration and control the flow of people based on national origins. Politicians had clear views about the proper immigrant mix they wished to produce. Preference would go to northern and western Europeans, not people from other parts of the world featuring individuals who looked or acted different.

With the onset of the Great Depression, neither Congress nor the general public was in any mood for open borders. Immigration dropped from 236,000 in 1929 to 23,000 in 1933. For the next decade, immigration averaged about 53,000 a year, dramatically lower than in earlier decades when hundreds of thousands of immigrants were arriving.[17]

The reality of a bad economy plus xenophobic feelings spawned by the Second World War encouraged elected leaders to further restrict foreign arrivals. The country no longer trusted people from countries against which it was fighting, such as Germans, Italians, and Japanese. Individuals of these nationalities were defined as untrustworthy, and no one wanted them to take American jobs or risk national security. After the 1941 Japanese attack on Pearl Harbor, internment camps were set up for Japanese already in the country. Two-thirds of the 120,000 imprisoned were American citizens. Their legal and constitutional rights were suspended, under an executive order issued by President Franklin Roosevelt in 1942 and upheld by the Supreme Court two years later.[18] German and Italian immigrants were not rounded up en masse but were subject to harassment and discrimination based on their ancestry.[19]

1965 LEGISLATION: FAMILY UNIFICATION ELEVATED

The closed-door regime remained in place for two decades following the end of World War II. It took a while for distrust of Japanese, Germans, and Italians in the United States to die down and for Americans to feel confident once again about the security of their borders. Concern over military security remained high in the aftermath of the global conflagration and the onset of the cold war.[20]

However, postwar prosperity and the need for new workers eventually paved the way for a shift in American policy back toward easier immigration. Public attitudes in the United States opened up gradually, and people began to see the virtues of foreign talent.

Culturally, American arts benefited from actors, dancers, and singers from other countries, while sports teams featured foreign-born talent. New restaurants emerged that specialized in French, Italian, Chinese, and Spanish cuisine and introduced native Americans to new foods and culinary approaches. Emigrés from European nations propelled American science and technology to global leadership. Scientists such as Albert Einstein and Enrico Fermi came to the United States in the 1930s, and their work was critical to America's postwar nuclear program. As the United States developed atomic weapons, intercontinental missiles, and a space program, foreign talent became especially important to national security and economic development.

The cold war had an impact as well. The pitched battle between capitalism and communism encouraged the United States to position itself as the land of freedom where people wanted to live and the Soviet Union as a place from which residents wanted to flee. The image of the Berlin Wall, which kept East Berliners contained while West Berliners prospered and thrived, sent a powerful message around the globe. Repressive regimes in the Soviet Union, China, and Cuba sent a similar message.

Having open borders became a powerful political message in the war against communism. Politically, Americans felt proud of the country as a beacon of liberty offering freedom of expression and opportunities for financial well-being to refugees from communist and authoritarian regimes. Economically, the United States portrayed itself as the land of opportunity. The idea of the American Dream once again expanded to include not just native-borns, but foreigners.

These attitudinal changes laid the groundwork for another fundamental change in U.S. immigration policy. In recognition of the fact that the previous century had seen the arrival of immigrants from around the world, the Hart-Celler Immigration and Nationality Act of 1965 abolished quotas based on national origins. Seventy percent of visas under the old system had gone to residents of the United Kingdom, Ireland, and Germany.[21] No longer would rigid limits be placed on the number of people eligible to immigrate to the United States from a particular country. Flexibility rather than rigidity became the governing feature.

In the place of national quotas, legislators for the first time elevated the principle of family reunification. Because many immigrants had arrived without their loved ones, the new policy gave priority to reuniting relatives. Bringing families together became a kind of civil rights or immigrant rights issue for advocates. No limits were placed on legal residents who wanted to bring in spouses, parents, or unmarried children under the age of eighteen. Never a major thrust of past American immigration regimes, family integration now became the centerpiece of national policy.

The 1965 legislation, which was adopted without much public clamor or rancor, had three major features.[22] First, it doubled the immigration ceiling from 150,000 to 290,000, with 170,000 visas for people from the Eastern Hemisphere and 120,000 for those from the West. Second, it gave explicit preference to family unification over employed-based requests. Naturalized citizens were eligible to bring their families into the country without being subject to the immigration ceilings. Third, it exempted spouses, children under the age of twenty-one, and parents over the age of twenty-one from numerical limits. Over time, these family unification provisions paved the way for what eventually became an average of more than a million new arrivals every year—many more people than initially envisioned under the overall immigration legislation.

Speaking on the floor of the House of Representatives, Representative Emanuel Celler (D-N.Y.) justified the bill's approach on antidiscrimination grounds. "With the end of discrimination due to place of birth, there will be shifts in countries other than those of northern and western Europe," he said. "Immigrants from Asia and Africa will have to compete and qualify in order to get in."[23] Attorney General Robert Kennedy praised the legislation, erroneously predicting that "the quota system [would] be replaced by the merit system."[24]

The legislation passed with huge majorities in the House and Senate. The vote was 326 to 69 in the House of Representatives, and 76 to 18 in the Senate. Befitting such a wholesale change in American policy, there were huge regional differences in legislative voting on this reform package. According to Martin Schain, 93 percent of northeastern representatives voted in support of the rewrite, compared with 27 percent of southern House members.[25] The Northeast was the part of the country housing large numbers of immigrants and their descendants, while the South had fewer immigrants and far more restrictionist attitudes to the general issue of immigration.

Demographic differences in congressional district characteristics help to explain legislative voting patterns. Rural areas and places in the South and Midwest had their doubts about this new policy. They continued to be concerned about cultural integration and national security threats. But with support from urban legislators and those from the two coasts, Congress overcame these partisan and regional barriers to construct a new national immigration strategy.

Legislators had the sense they were restoring fairness and merit selection to American immigration. They confidently predicted there would be no major change in ethnic composition or a big spike in overall immigration numbers. Senator Edward M. Kennedy, the chair of the immigration subcommittee, predicted that "our cities will not be flooded with a million immigrants annually."[26] Representative Celler anticipated that "there will not be, comparatively, many Asians or Africans entering this country. . . . Since the people of Africa and Asia have very few relatives here, comparatively few could immigrate from those countries because they have no family ties in the U.S."[27] Signing the legislation at the Statue of Liberty on October 3, 1965, President Lyndon Johnson played down its likely effect: "This bill we sign today is not a revolutionary bill. It does not affect the lives of millions. It will not restructure the shape of our daily lives."[28]

The immigration reform was motivated largely on humanitarian grounds. After all, husbands wished to be reunited with their wives, parents with children, and grandchildren with grandparents, aunts, and uncles. It made sense to have policies that encouraged family unity. Policymakers saw great value in a "pro-family" perspective, both from a political and policy standpoint.

In addition, building strong families was important for promoting a variety of desirable social outcomes. Family integration was associated with neighborhood stability, positive education outcomes, and economic prosperity. More family members often meant more income and more family stability. Powerful arguments suggested that successful child rearing required parents and close relatives to be active participants in kids' upbringing.[29]

For example, research on domestic "broken homes" suggested that children from divided families were more likely to resort to crime and violence than were children with the nurturing benefits of a family environment.[30] In his analysis of juvenile delinquency, Michael Wadsworth concluded that "the most striking finding concerned family life, where disruption of parent-child relationships in early life, through parental death, divorce or separation, was associated with later delinquency, and chiefly with the most unacceptable kinds of offenses."[31]

Other analysts noted the benefit of family integration for how children turned out. A project undertaken by Jackson Toby found that the loss of parental control was detrimental to children's social behavior. "The better integrated the family, the more successful it is as a bulwark against anti-social influences emanating from the neighborhood or the peer group," he argued.[32] A variety of indicators suggested that children raised by two parents in a cohesive social fabric were more likely to graduate from high school, attend college, and have successful careers than those who did not.

By making the principle of family unity so central to public policy, however, authorities fundamentally altered the dynamics of future immigration. The act created the unanticipated consequence of what has become known as "chain immigration." Under this process, one family member arrived in the United States, gained legal status, and then sponsored his or her spouse, children, parents, brothers, and sisters for legal status. The chain started by one family member led to numerous relatives coming to America. Instead of deciding who should be allowed to gain entry based on national goals, policymakers created an automatic process by which blood ties determined entry into the United States.

Essentially, the United States moved to a system where relatives, not national policymakers, determined who could immigrate to the United States.

It was perfectly understandable that families would exploit this provision of the law. What started as a trickle of family members became a flood as individuals used family reunification as the route to bringing loved ones to rejoin them in America. Without much public understanding of how dramatically the country had altered its approach to immigration and contrary to the predictions of prominent politicians of the day, legislators had created a new approach with a very different principle at its core than ever had been the case in American history.

Eventually, this policy altered the balance between entry based on family ties versus occupational preferences. In 1970, for example, five years after this new policy was adopted but before its ramifications were fully understood, entry linked to occupational preferences still constituted 60 percent of the quota ceiling. As more and more immigrants began to take advantage of the family reunification preference, occupational preferences began to drop, falling to 17 percent of the total in 1978.[33]

By 1996, when the new policy was in full force and well understood among the immigrant community, the U.S. Immigration and Naturalization Service allowed 911,000 immigrants to come to America. Sixty-six percent (or 595,000 individuals) entered based on family reunification, compared to 12 percent (118,000 people) for job skills and 22 percent (198,000 individuals) based on humanitarian reasons.[34]

In 2008, the most recent year for which there are data, 1,107,126 legal permanent residents were admitted to the United States. Of these, 64 percent (716,244) were family-sponsored; 15 percent (166,511) were employment-based; 19 percent (208,153) were granted refugee status or political asylum or were given diversity admissions; and the rest (2 percent) fell into other categories. Among those coming to America because of family ties, the majority were spouses, children, and parents of immigrants; a much smaller percentage were brothers and sisters and adult children of legal permanent residents.[35]

In short, the priority given to family reunification overwhelmed all other objectives set out in the 1965 legislation. Even though legislators stated that the overall number of immigrants would not change much, because relatives did not count against quotas, the numbers increased from 290,000 entries to more than 1 million a year.

Around the same time, the ethnic mix of new arrivals shifted toward Latin Americans, Asians, and Africans. This distinctive character of these new arrivals had a profound impact on American public opinion, with some Americans having great difficulty welcoming immigrants who looked very different from themselves. Fear and resentment of ethnically and racially different immigrants soon led to public debates over immigration that took on controversial and highly emotional elements.

Lawmakers were slow to recognize the long-term impact of their policy choices. As in many other policy areas, unanticipated consequences became the most important ramification of the new legislation. First, America ended up with a far higher volume of immigrants than anticipated under the congressional legislation. Second, the bill made it difficult for the United States to recruit foreign individuals with the special skills needed for innovation, economic development, or entrepreneurial growth. Although some of those admitted under family unification became entrepreneurs and made economic contributions, their entry was based on family ties as opposed to economic potential. With a national policy that did not clearly identify or target desired benefits, the legislation sowed the long-term seeds for popular disenchantment with contemporary immigration policy. The flood of legal—and illegal—immigrants and their extended families fueled populist anger and made many people doubt the overall benefits of immigration.

PROBLEMS OF THE CURRENT IMMIGRATION REGIME

As a humanitarian principle, family reunification works very effectively. It brings relatives together. The policy has the benefits of being profamily, promarriage, and prochildren. Immigrants themselves are overjoyed that they can earn the financial and material benefits of coming to America without leaving behind their spouses, children, and parents. At the personal level, this policy makes great sense and helps the United States build strong families.

The problem, though, is that this near-exclusive emphasis on family unification ignores other important priorities such as American competitiveness, human capital, border security, crime prevention, entrepreneurship, and economic innovation. The overwhelming number of visas devoted to new family members means very few visas are available for seasonal workers, scientists and engineers, or foreign graduates of American universities and makes it politically difficult to expand the number of visas in nonfamily categories.

As I note below, current policy defines "family" too broadly and does not address immigration fears linked to crime, health, or border security. Because immigration policy does not deal effectively with many of the issues that concern the American public, maintaining public support for immigration becomes difficult, and building political coalitions in support of policies that further long-term national objectives is nearly impossible. Americans simply grow more cynical about the ability of the government to enforce existing immigration policies.

The Need to Invest in Human Capital and Economic Competitiveness

America has a glaring shortage of native-born scientists and engineers. Research on the national origins of American science and engineering Ph.D.s demonstrates big changes over the past several decades. In 1966, for example, 77 percent of all those individuals in the United States with advanced graduate degrees were born in the United States, while 23 percent were foreign-born. By 2000 the American-born number had dropped to 61 percent, while the foreign-born figure had risen to 39 percent.[36]

Each year American universities train more than half a million international students.[37] These individuals come from all around the globe to advance their learning and job skills. They see U.S. schools as among the best in the world and want to train with the top leaders in various fields. Many of these graduates would like to stay in the United States and get jobs or develop businesses. Salaries are typically higher in America than in their native countries, and the benefits are better. In addition, many international graduates like the freedom of expression, cultural enrichment, and standard of living found in the United States.

Although universities invest billions in paying for the tuitions of these individuals, the country does little to reap the rewards of this investment. Even though many foreign students are attracted to the United States, most new graduates go home because they cannot obtain work permits such as green cards and therefore qualify for positions here. It takes years to navigate the immigration process, and the only way to get a scarce H-1B visa is to be sponsored by a major American company such as Microsoft, Yahoo, Hewlett-Packard, IBM, or Google.[38]

Foreign seasonal farm workers encounter a similar problem. American agriculture relies on foreign workers to pick fruit, harvest crops, and gather vegetables. Indeed, demand for these employees is extensive. In 1998, 21,594 Mexican agricultural workers came to the United States under the H-2A visa; by 2006 this number had nearly doubled to 40,283, reflecting increased demands in this area. Similar increases have occurred in regard to the H-2B visa program for nonagricultural seasonal workers. In 1998, 10,727 unskilled Mexican laborers entered America on H-2B visas, but by 2006 this number had risen to 89,184.[39]

These visa programs are vital for economic competitiveness because most American workers are unwilling to undertake this kind of work for the wages paid.[40] Farm owners have complained for years about problems of hiring native-born people willing to work in the fields. These jobs are physically demanding and short term in nature, limiting their attractiveness to people already in the country. The jobs do not pay well and rarely offer health or retirement benefits, so farmers face challenges in recruiting a sufficient supply of able employees.

Clearly there is a trade-off in existing policy between visas for family reunification versus occupational positions. The relatively low number of work visas (about 15 percent of the total in 2008) limits the ability of the United States to maintain international competitiveness or develop the talent needed for long-term economic development.

An Overly Broad Definition of Family

The definition of "family" in current policy is overly broad. The family unity principle makes sense in regard to immediate relatives, where a substantial body of research demonstrates a strong tie between immediate families and social well-being, economic outcomes, and educational attainment. There is little doubt that strong families produce good societal results.[41]

But this rationale is much weaker when applied to extended families. Little evidence shows that having aunts, uncles, or cousins around limits divorce, encourages educational achievement, or leads to higher family incomes. There are no compelling data for kinship ties based on more distant relatives. All of the purported advantages are based on parental upbringing, not extended relationships.[42]

Nor is there a moral imperative for bringing relatives other than spouses, children, and parents to America, absent a need for political asylum or protection from a civil war or repressive authoritarian government. When people come to America of their own free will, they make a conscious decision to leave behind various relatives. It makes little sense to base U.S. policy on the ramifications of these personal choices when there is a clear opportunity cost in terms of other types of entrants. It is akin to leaving your parents behind in another nation and then asking for preferential treatment on grounds that you are a de facto orphan.

If family-based immigration were limited to the immediate relatives of U.S. citizens, it would free up hundreds of thousands of visas to be used to attract individuals with special talents or skills needed by American businesses. Limiting family-based immigration represents a way to rebalance immigration policy and to accommodate several important policy objectives.

Inadequate Attention to Crime or Border Security

One of the chief objections Americans have toward immigration is inadequate border security and the large number of illegal aliens who live in the United States. For example, a Pew Research Center survey in 2009 that asked people about their biggest concern regarding immigration found that the four main worries were loss of American jobs to immigrants (34 percent), increased danger of terrorism (20 percent), increased crime (14 percent), and negative effects on the American way of life (10 percent).[43]

Despite the widespread and vocal public concern about illegal immigration, the total budget for the U.S. Border Patrol was $1.2 billion in 2004 and now stands just under $2 billion (not including the money currently spent on fencing and monitoring equipment).[44] Compared with the amount spent administering the rest of the immigration system, this figure is clearly inadequate to reassure the American public that the administration has secured the borders and protected native-born citizens from illegal aliens, crime, and threats to personal health. Unless national authorities devote greater resources to issues that are on the public's mind, it will be difficult to reassure citizens that current policy is on the right track.

Difficulty of Building Political Coalitions

The widespread dissatisfaction with virtually every aspect of immigration policy makes that policy difficult to support politically. The United States has an unbalanced policy that tilts far too heavily in the direction of family integration to the virtual exclusion of other goals such as economic competitiveness, investing in human capital, and protecting national borders. An unsatisfactory status quo also makes it difficult to build a coalition in favor of immigration reform. When the current policy works poorly, people are unwilling to believe that a new policy can be run any more effectively. The resulting spiral of cynicism perpetuates an unpopular status quo and low citizen confidence that a future immigration regime would do any better.

What is needed in this situation is an immigration policy that provides a better balance between family and economic goals and that promotes innovation and economic development. The United States should use its scarce visas to recruit top talent and attract individuals that enhance its long-term economic, cultural, and intellectual life. Finding the next Sergey Brin, Andrew Grove, or Mikhail Baryshnikov would improve the national economy, enhance the American culture, and increase the country's ability to compete internationally.

Not only would such a shift in policy be good for the long-term economy, it would increase political support for immigration policy. The American public tends to be very "bottom-line" oriented in its assessments. If policies produce stronger outcomes, citizens will feel better about new arrivals. They would be less cynical about existing policy if the benefits of immigration policy were more clearly defined. But it will take fundamental reforms to produce a bottom-line that is acceptable to the general public.

CHAPTER THREE

OVERCOMING PARTICULARISTIC POLITICS

IMMIGRATION IS A TOPIC THAT arouses strong passions in nearly every part of the political spectrum. Because the issue involves questions of culture, language, economics, social mores, and national character, debates over competing policy objectives are rarely calm and rational. Expressions of fear, anxiety, and anger are more typical than reason-based discussions.[1] People commonly question motives, disparage opponents, and make jingoistic arguments when analyzing the nature of immigration policy in the United States, making it hard to address political controversies meaningfully. A substantial number of Americans are opposed to immigration and to government policies that are sympathetic to newcomers.[2]

Even during good economic times, changing immigration law is a major challenge. Beyond the emotional character of the debate, immigration reform legislation faces many political and institutional challenges. The American governance system features many veto points in the legislative branch.[3] The decentralized structure of Congress weakens decisionmaking because authority is divided between different committees and subcommittees. The tendency for individual members of Congress to emphasize local concerns undermines consideration of broader and long-term national interests.[4]

Policymaking problems are not unique to the immigration area. As witnessed in recent years, large-scale reform is difficult on subjects from health care and trade agreements to climate change. The nation's founders intentionally designed a governmental system that was slow to move and required a strong political consensus to make changes. Based on their treatment by the British monarchy during colonial times, they mistrusted centralized political institutions and feared excessive concentration of political power.[5] They wanted legislators to go through a long deliberative process on major issues to avoid hasty decisions.[6]

But the combination of fragmented institutions, decentralized decisionmaking, localized politics, and an emotionally fraught issue has stymied comprehensive immigration reform in recent decades. In today's climate, marked by political polarization, economic slowdown, and worry about terrorist threats from abroad, navigating a divided political system and assembling a winning legislative coalition can seem all but impossible.[7] Bad economies increase people's anxieties and make them worry about foreign competition. When a recession is thrown on top of polarized politics and competing jurisdictions, the political situation deteriorates rapidly and needed immigration reforms become very difficult to enact.[8]

Anxieties about the impact of immigrants help explain why the United States often has adopted immigration policies that were misguided, short-sighted, or outright discriminatory. The times when immigration has proven most contentious have been during periods when new arrivals spawned fears about loss of national character, threats to national security, and lack of social integration. For evidence, one need look only at the exclusion of the Chinese during the nineteenth century, the internment of Japanese Americans during World War II, the suspicions with which Mexicans and other Hispanic immigrants are often treated today, and the distrust of Arab immigrants following the September 11, 2001, terrorist attacks.

Indeed, American history is strewn with examples of two very different forms of ineffective decisionmaking regarding immigration. At times elected officials have clearly overreacted to specific episodes or jingoistic political environments and thereby made hasty and ill-begotten decisions. At other times, stalemate and inaction have prevented political leaders from addressing needed reforms even when people were unhappy with the status quo.

Policy overreactions are problematic because decisions are based on short-term considerations that do not serve long-term priorities. As a result, U.S. policy lurches from one direction to another, with little stability or predictability. Policy inaction is equally problematic because it prevents leaders from resolving social conflicts or addressing important problems. Instead, the status quo remains in effect even as problems grow worse.[9] People complain about many different aspects of immigration policy, but political stalemate makes it impossible to address any element of the situation.

For these reasons, the history of American immigration policy does not show the United States political system at its best. Fragmented institutions and emotional policy responses have damaged America's national policy interests and led to irrational decisions. Because these have been long-standing problems in the United States, policymakers and citizens alike need to address the various political and institutional problems that prevent legislators from enacting more reasonable policies.[10]

POLITICAL AND INSTITUTIONAL CHARACTERISTICS

Political features matter a lot in the conduct and resolution of public sector decisionmaking. The particular combination of formal and informal mechanisms, centralized or decentralized processes, national versus local considerations, and the rational or emotional character of deliberations has enormous consequences for the end result in the policy process.

These characteristics influence everything from how discussions are structured to the manner in which issues are decided.[11] They have ramifications for agenda formation, legislative consideration, policy passage, and administrative implementation. Often, they are the determining force in how policy controversies are resolved.[12]

For example, education is a decentralized domain with local school districts holding much of the authority. Schools are financed by local property taxes and governed through locally elected school boards.[13] Parents care deeply about the curriculum, after-school activities, food service, and teacher qualifications. In a situation of extensive local control and neighborhood interest, the federal government has relatively little leverage to drive change and shape the way in which public preferences are compiled. This fact shapes the overall contours of education policy.

In immigration policy the politics tend to be parochial, emotional, and particularistic. For most of American history, Congress has been the primary decisionmaking body on this issue. Legislative decisions take place in a fragmented and decentralized institution. The House of Representatives was created by the founders as the "people's" body. Its 435 members are elected every two years, providing regular opportunities for public feedback. Legislators make policy decisions in subcommittees, committees, and on the floor, and are very sensitive to local considerations.

Senators have six-year terms, but the Senate remains a relatively decentralized chamber as well, with individual senators quite responsive to constituents, especially on controversial subjects where public opinion is divided.[14] The Senate's decisionmaking processes revolve around committees and subcommittees, and individual senators have much greater latitude than do members of the House to use procedural maneuvers to tie up action. A chief procedural tool in recent years for opponents of legislation has been the filibuster—talking a bill or amendment to death unless at least sixty of the one hundred members vote to stop the discussion.

This fragmented, decentralized, and particularistic legislative structure works against making decisions in a coherent or calm manner. Congressional discussions of immigration have often been largely emotional and filled with highly charged rhetoric about the dangers immigrants might cause to American social, economic, and political life. Given its responsiveness to public opinion and outside pressures, Congress has repeatedly found it difficult, if not impossible, to deliberate calmly and resolve major policy differences. In such circumstances, those who stake out extreme positions often hold sway, even if such positions prevent Congress from taking action.[15]

Past immigration debates have been clearly characterized by particularistic and emotional politics that have hindered decision-making. Problems of institutional structure, overheated rhetoric, and polarized politics have resulted in failed policies, overreactions, and policy stalemates that have not advanced America's long-term interests. The following pages examine three of these debates in greater detail.

MISGUIDED DECISIONS: THE CHINESE EXCLUSION ACT OF 1882

The history of legislative action on immigration shows the limits of particularistic politics in complex policy areas. In examining the evolution of American immigration policy, it is clear that politics has driven policy in undesirable ways. One of the country's most short-sighted and racist decisions was the Chinese Exclusion Act of 1882, one of the few times in American history in which immigration policy targeted a specific ethnic group for exclusion.[16]

The exclusion legislation reflected popular animosity toward Chinese immigrants that had begun several decades earlier. Between 1857 and 1882, around 228,000 Chinese were recruited by railroad companies to migrate to the United States, where they clustered mainly on the West Coast. San Francisco was a major gathering place for Chinese immigrants, who arrived at the city's large port, got jobs, and then encouraged family members and friends to follow their path. Chinese immigrants produced boots and shoes, cleaned homes, and set up laundry businesses; many went to work helping to build the transcontinental railroad.

Although America generally had open borders during this period, the arrival of the Chinese immigrants sparked a substantial backlash among native-born Americans. Cities often forced the immigrants to live in "Chinatown" ghettos, and many were subjected to vigilante violence.[17] News reports of the day describe Chinese being attacked on the sidewalks and even in their homes; a number were killed or seriously injured. In California an anti-immigration group called the Supreme Order of Caucasians formed in 1876 to fight Chinese immigration. It opened sixty-four chapters around the state and recruited nearly 5,000 members.[18]

Not surprisingly, given the virulence of anti-Chinese sentiments among the general public as a whole, politicians responded with discriminatory measures. The California legislature made several attempts to restrict Chinese immigration. It enacted a bill requiring each new arrival to be vaccinated and charged $10 for the medical service. However, this measure was struck down by the courts. Legislators also outlawed the Chinese custom of wearing pigtails, only to have that restriction struck down as well. Another piece of legislation attempted to facilitate the eviction of Chinese from rental homes "by condemning their property in bulk as a nuisance," but this too was invalidated. Other bills sought to restrict Chinese employment options to specified activities and to outline conditions under which they could wash dirty clothes. But judicial authorities found these measures to represent illegal restrictions on a single group.[19]

The backlash was not restricted to the West Coast. In 1871 Representative William M. (Boss) Tweed introduced a bill into the New York state legislature to "prohibit the employment of any 'heathen Chinese' or coolly laborer in the State of New York." Individuals who hired Chinese "to build railroads, grade streets, make boots and shoes, or perform other labor" would be subject to a civil fine of between $1,000 and $5,000, imprisonment between six and twelve months, or both. *Harper's* editorialized against this bill, writing that "the Chinese invasion, of which [Tweed] seems to be so much afraid, is altogether mythical."[20]

With the courts overturning many state and local restrictions, public opinion grew more and more inflamed. Over a period of several years, the political climate laid the groundwork for Congress to pass the U.S. Chinese Exclusion Act of 1882. This bill prohibited the entry of any new Chinese workers into America after the passage of the legislation, although Chinese already in the country were allowed to remain. The House overwhelmingly passed the bill, 179-43, while the Senate approved it on a more narrow margin of 39 to 27. These restrictions remained in place until 1943, when they were repealed by Congress during the Second World War.

Even after the federal legislation was enacted, discrimination against Chinese continued. In 1890, for example, a San Francisco supervisor named Bingham introduced an ordinance calling for the "removal of Chinatown." The *Wave* newspaper criticized the proposed ordinance, saying "we seem to be trying to beat our past record in fanatical persecution of the Chinese." Its editorial pointed out the gross injustice of a bill outlawing gambling in Chinatown, while allowing it elsewhere around the city. [21]

OVERREACTION: THE RESPONSE TO 9/11

The government's response to the 9/11 terrorist attacks demonstrates another case of policy overreaction. There is no question that these attacks shocked Americans and required a strong policy response. People were terrified by the hijacking of passenger aircraft that were then flown into the World Trade Center in New York City and the Pentagon, killing 2,974 individuals. Even as the attacks were unfolding live before people's eyes on national television, demands to identify the perpetrators and protect America from further attacks were already being heard.[22]

The administration quickly identified the al Qaeda terrorist organization as the sponsor of the attacks, in which it recruited nineteen young male Arabs for the suicide mission. Fifteen of the hijackers came from Saudi Arabia, two from the United Arab Emirates, one from Egypt, and one from Lebanon.

The use of foreigners to launch attacks within the United States stimulated much thinking about border control and immigration processes. Some of the attackers entered America on student visas, so heightened scrutiny was given to criteria for approving these kinds of applications. Others had overstayed the expiration date on their American visas, spurring calls for greater efforts to find and expel those foreigners who abuse entry programs.[23]

Shortly after the attacks, President George W. Bush declared a "war on terrorism" and, within a month, convinced Congress to pass the USA Patriot Act, an acronym standing for Uniting and Strengthening America by Providing Appropriate Tools Required to Intercept and Obstruct Terrorism Act of 2001. Among other provisions, it authorized law enforcement agencies to search American citizens' personal records for intelligence-gathering purposes and adopted tough rules allowing government officials to track financial transactions, e-mail, and phone conversations linked to foreigners.

Most important for the immigration area, the legislative bill tightened border security and strenghtened procedures for "detaining and deporting immigrants suspected of terrorism-related acts." A number were detained and deported for immigration violations.[24] It provided for more thorough background checks on those wishing to come to America, authorized mandatory detention of suspected terrorists, and required use of new biometric identification tools for new arrivals. U.S. consulates around the world were instructed to undertake detailed personal interviews as part of the visa application process. This step was designed to help agents identify why visitors wanted to come to the United States and whether they represented any threat to the country.

More controversially, the act streamlined deportation proceedings so that it was easier to expel foreigners who overstayed visas, committed crimes in America, lied on applications, or otherwise engaged in undesirable activities. If someone fell into one of these categories, they could be scheduled for deportation and, after a court hearing, physically removed from the United States.[25]

Over the past decade, deportations averaged around 250,000 annually. This constitutes about one-quarter of the new legal arrivals each year. Legislators beefed up border enforcement, created a Department of Homeland Security, and authorized much tougher security procedures. The goal was to promote a stronger defense for America and ensure that no further attacks took place.

The Patriot Act created huge complications for colleges and universities seeking to admit foreign students. Around 500,000 foreign students attend American universities every year. Because admission decisions typically are made in April for classes that start in September, accepted students have only a four-month window to apply for student visas, get processed by their local consulate, submit relevant fingerprints and biometrics, pass a personal interview, and obtain the visa. Since the new screening procedures went into effect, a number of foreign students have not received their visa in time to enroll in classes. Not only was this traumatic for the student involved, it created problems for colleges and universities who counted on these pupils enrolling in their programs. It complicates admission decisions when institutions of higher learning are not sure which students will get visas. New York mayor Michael Bloomberg complained that "after 9/11 we went from reaching out and trying to get the best and the brightest to come here, to trying to keep them out."[26]

The tough application process also created difficulties for businesses wanting to bring workers to the United States. The long time frames required for visa processing and the arduous procedures for complying with entry provisions are particularly problematic for seasonal workers. Workers are needed when crops are ready for harvesting, not two weeks or two months later. Businesses requiring highly skilled workers face similar time constraints:

when high-tech firms have code to write or equipment to manufacture, they needs scientists and engineers right then.

The rigors of the Patriot Act have turned immigration into an
area where many sectors are unhappy with the tight restrictions.
Businesses and educational institutions find the new requirements
overly burdensome and time-consuming. New paperwork rules for
student and employee visas are onerous and difficult to complete
in a timely manner.[27] Foreign visitors resent new rules requiring
fingerprints even for routine tourist visits. Some countries, such
as Brazil, retaliated by enacting the same types of requirements
for Americans visiting their nation. The breadth and depth of
these reactions reveal the intensity of the resentment found among
many different people in the United States and around the world.

INACTION AND STALEMATE:
THE FAILURE OF COMPREHENSIVE REFORM IN 2006 AND 2007

Widespread unhappiness with the immigration status quo fueled
interest in undertaking comprehensive immigration reform during
Bush's second term. A variety of businesses were unhappy with
inadequate access to low- and high-skilled workers. Labor unions
felt that worker wages were compromised by foreign competition
and that American employees were being harmed. Those concerned about border security fretted about the large number of
undocumented aliens crossing the border between Mexico and
the United States. Hispanic groups complained about raids of
workplaces that penalized the employees but not the employers.

In his second term, President George W. Bush and a bipartisan
team of congressional leaders staked out compromise legislation
that sought to meld the best of liberal and conservative perspectives on immigration. These individuals sought to address the
concerns of conservatives about border security by increasing
enforcement and building fences along the Mexican boundary.
Liberals wanted a path to citizenship for illegal immigrants who
had been in the country a long time, so the proposed bill provided

a means to do this if the individual paid a fine and back taxes. The act sought to enlist business support by raising the number of guest workers who could be admitted to the United States through a new visa program.

The chief executive devoted serious effort to trying to build a coalition in favor of this bill. He met with conservatives within his own party, asking for their help with the legislation. He gave major speeches on the value of immigration reform. He saw comprehensive legislation as key to rebuilding better relationships with Mexico and Latin America. Speaking at a joint press conference with Mexican President Felipe Calderón, for example, Bush said, "A good migration law will help both economies and will help the security of both countries. If people can come into our country, for example, on a temporary basis to work, doing jobs Americans aren't doing, they won't have to sneak across the border."[28]

Not only did the president see policy merits in this action, there was a political rationale as well. With the growing size and activism of Hispanics in electoral politics, Bush wanted to continue the gains Republicans had made in that constituency in recent years. In 2004, for example, Republicans had garnered 40 percent of the Hispanic vote in the presidential election, their best showing in years.[29] With 46 million Hispanics in the United States, this constituency represented a major opportunity for the GOP. The president's brother, Jeb Bush, recognized the crucial political value of Latinos when he noted that "the swing voters are Hispanic voters in most of the swing states."[30] While this statement reflected optimism that Republicans could increase their percentage of the Hispanic vote, it also demonstrated the hope that immigration reform would bring the GOP electoral benefits.

Despite the president's efforts and bipartisan support from a number of influential legislators, Congress failed to pass the legislation two years in a row. In 2006 the Senate passed legislation cosponsored by Edward M. Kennedy (D-Mass.) and John McCain (R-Ariz.) that would have increased border security, established a temporary guest worker program, and set up a path to citizenship for many illegal immigrants. But the bill died in the House after Republicans refused to consider what many of them described as an amnesty bill.

In 2007 Kennedy and McCain again introduced comprehensive legislation reform legislation that had Bush's support. Called the Secure Borders, Economic Opportunity and Immigration Reform Act of 2007, the legislation was similar to that passed in 2006, with a few changes designed to attract additional support from some legislators who had opposed the 2006 measure.

Both liberals and conservatives attacked the legislation. Liberals were not happy about spending money to build hundreds of miles of border fencing or with restrictions placed on immigrants already in the United States. They also said the guest worker program would undermine American workers and depress wages.

Conservatives again bemoaned what they called "amnesty" for illegal immigrants and voiced fears that immigrants would draw more than their share of taxpayer-funded public services. There was tough talk about illegal immigrants overrunning America and destroying the economic, social, and cultural character of the country. In addition, a number of senators felt strongly that the legislation was poorly devised and would not improve the immigration situation. Three GOP senators, James DeMint of South Carolina, Jeff Sessions of Alabama, and David Vitter of Louisiana filibustered the bill, using a variety of legislative and procedural tactics to delay consideration of the legislation.[31] Senate leaders were unable to garner the necessary sixty votes needed to stop the Republican filibuster, which effectively killed the legislation.

Several political and institutional obstacles doomed this legislation. First, an unlikely coalition of conservatives worried about border security and liberals worried about competition for jobs and the long route to citizenship for illegal immigrants combined to defeat the legislation. On an emotional subject featuring lots of fear and fearmongering, it is difficult to build the legislative support required for congressional action. As envisioned by the founders, congressional legislation is easier to stop than to enact.

In a 2008 Brookings report, writer E. J. Dionne noted the substantive problems various groups saw with the proposal. He described the vast array of opponents as "growers seeking seasonal farmworkers; high-tech firms seeking engineers; libertarians opposed to national identity documents; proponents of rigorous enforcement measures; Asian groups preoccupied with family visas, Latino groups preoccupied with legalization for the undocumented, others preoccupied with refugees and particular nationalities; unions wanting to grow by organizing immigrants and unions wanting to protect their existing members from competition with immigrants."[32]

The multifaceted nature of the opposition made it difficult to overcome differences and build support for a specific bill. With each group fearful about some specific aspect of the legislation and unwilling to compromise on that key principle, an untenable political situation was created. Senators were not able to resolve these disputes, and the legislation was defeated by a classic "coalition of political minorities" consisting of many small pockets opposed to specific provisions.

Institutional factors also played a key role in Senate discussions. Because of the sixty-vote requirement for ending a filibuster, the Senate in effect needed a supermajority to move the legislation. In all likelihood, a bill could have been enacted if only a simple majority had been needed for passage. The sixty-vote requirement is a high hurdle to cross on any controversial subject, and for immigration reform it proved too high.

Other factors were also involved. The debate was colored by extreme political polarization, emotional rhetoric, and divisive and strident media coverage. The fragmented nature of Congress and members' strong orientation to local concerns enabled advocates on each side of the political aisle to torpedo legislation that sought to address fundamental problems. It was easier to kick the immigration problem down the road to a future Congress than to come up with a workable solution to a serious problem. Despite the support of a conservative president who sought a bipartisan compromise with legislators of different viewpoints, lawmakers could not build sufficient support to pass the legislation.

OPPORTUNITIES TO OVERCOME PAROCHIALISM

The 2008 elections ushered in a different political landscape that gave proponents hope that the country might be ready to overcome its typical parochialism and move toward comprehensive immigration reform. The most striking feature of the new terrain was a popular Democratic president armed with substantial Democratic majorities in the House and Senate. Unified party control of the national government does not guarantee large-scale policymaking, however. Democrats controlled Congress and the presidency during the Carter administration but were unable to reform energy policy, a top priority for that administration. During President Bill Clinton's first two years in office, Democrats were in a similarly strong political position, yet failed to enact his top priority, comprehensive health care reform.

Nonetheless, on contentious subjects requiring intricate compromise, it helps to have one party clearly in charge. This institutional position makes it easier to negotiate policy differences because it narrows the range of principles that must be negotiated. Members of one party typically share certain values and principles. Bargaining with like-minded lawmakers narrows the ideas that are compromised. That is especially the case during periods of extreme polarization of the sort witnessed in recent years, when each party is striving for electoral advantage and extremes within each group are demanding pure responses. But the range of political principles among current Democratic legislators is substantial, which limits the ability to reach consensus on legislative action.

The new landscape also appeared favorable to reform because it brought in a new administration that focused on big ideas and bold policy actions. The 2008 election took place against a backdrop of a global recession, faltering financial institutions, and a strong sense among the American public that old policy approaches were failing and new ones were required. A CBS News/*New York Times* national survey found that in October 2008 only 7 percent of Americans thought the country was headed in the right direction, while 89 percent felt it was seriously off on the wrong track.

With massive public discontent and big Democratic majorities, President Barack Obama pledged a new policy course in areas from financial regulation and education to health care and energy. As reflected in the American Recovery and Reinvestment Act of 2009, the new administration showed a willingness to tackle tough issues and try new policy approaches. In his inaugural address, Obama promised to alter the status quo. Noting that critics had complained that he had "too many big plans," the chief executive responded that "the ground has shifted" and it was time for a "new era of responsibility."

On immigration reform, the president expressed strong support for comprehensive legislation. At a March 18, 2009, town hall meeting in Costa Mesa, California, he explained that "I know this is an emotional issue, I know it's a controversial issue, I know that the people get real riled up politically about this, but—but ultimately, here's what I believe: We are a nation of immigrants. . . . I don't think that we can do this piecemeal." During an April 29, 2009, press conference, the president reiterated his desire to move the process forward: "We can't continue with a broken immigration system. It's not good for anybody. It's not good for American workers. It's dangerous for Mexican would-be workers who are trying to cross a dangerous border."

The Obama administration benefited from experienced leaders in key departments. For example, Secretary Janet Napolitano of Homeland Security is a former governor of Arizona who brings detailed immigration knowledge and political skills to the national government. Commerce Secretary Gary Locke is an

Asian American who as governor of Washington presided over a state with considerable in-migration, especially from Asian countries. Top Democratic leaders in Congress also said they were committed to action on immigration. At a 2009 San Francisco rally, House Speaker Nancy Pelosi (D-Calif.) complained about raids targeting illegal aliens. "Who in this country would not want to change a policy of kicking in doors in the middle of the night and sending a parent away from their families?" She said she had urged Obama "to stop the misguided raids and deportations that are tearing [apart] marriages, children and families." And Senate Majority Leader Harry Reid (D-Nev.) had long supported the Dream Act and other initiatives that would allow "students who have lived in the country since age 15 to apply for conditional legal residence after graduating from high school." So, although reform is never easy to enact, the country appeared to have an unusual opportunity to take decisive action on immigration.

But the Great Recession of 2008 and 2009 complicated execution of these wishes. In short order, unemployment rose to 10 percent and the president's popularity dropped. As they had in previous economic downturns, American citizens grew anxious about immigrants taking their jobs and angry with their political leaders. At the same time, Congress bogged down over health care reform. Although both chambers passed health bills, with virtually no Republican support, the differences between them were so great that it was unclear whether Democrats could agree on a compromise measure they could pass without some Republican support. When Massachusetts Republican Scott Brown won a special election in early 2010 to fill the Senate seat held by the late Edward M. Kennedy, Senate Democrats lost their sixty-vote supermajority, jeopardizing their ability to overcome GOP filibusters. The majority party's struggle to find consensus among its members on health care boded ill for consensus on equally contentious issues such as climate change and immigration reform, while the approaching midterm elections in November 2010 also made scheduling debate on reform legislation problematic.

When health care reform eventually passed Congress in 2010 and was signed into law by President Obama, it created the opportunity for legislators to think about other issues. As part of health reform, President Obama promised Hispanic legislators that he would speed action on immigration reform. He gave several speeches promoting comprehensive legislation and urged Congress to take action. But like other presidents, he found it difficult to navigate the emotion-laden political environment surrounding immigration. Passage of a state law affecting immigrants made the political environment even more complicated.

In spring 2010 the Arizona legislature enacted a tough border enforcement law, stimulating calls for immigration reform. The legislation's emphasis on permitting local police to ask for legal documentation of anyone suspected of being in the state illegally fueled complaints that the bill would encourage racial profiling of Hispanics. Concerned about the draconian approach, Latinos held protests across the country demanding congressional action to improve immigration policy and foreclose other states from following Arizona's example.[33]

At the same time, a CBS News/*New York Times* survey found that more Americans wanted the national government to set immigration policy. When asked whether laws regarding illegal immigration should be determined by the federal or state government, 57 percent said they thought it should be set at the federal level, while 34 percent believed state government should determine the policy.[34]

When asked specifically about the Arizona law, 82 percent said in this survey they thought the legislation would be very or somewhat likely to lead policy officers to detain people of certain racial or ethnic groups more frequently than others. Only 15 percent felt it would not encourage racial profiling. But many (69 percent) thought the law would be effective at deterring people from other countries from illegally crossing the border into Arizona.

However, the arrest of Faisal Shahzad, a naturalized U.S. citizen from Pakistan, on charges of attempting to detonate a gasoline and propane-filled SUV in New York City's Times Square leveled the political playing field. The fact that he had migrated from abroad raised security considerations that emboldened critics to argue that immigration reform would bring more foreigners to the United States and that this would be dangerous for American safety.[35]

Growing Latino Power

In the long run, a factor that potentially favors immigration reform is the changing demography of the American electorate. Nationally, the Latino population constitutes 15 percent of the total population, up from 12 percent in 2000. With 46 million Hispanic citizens, the group is a rising political power. That is especially the case because they are concentrated in several key states—New Mexico (44 percent of the state population), California (36 percent), Texas (36 percent), Arizona (30 percent), and Nevada (25 percent).

Hispanics were crucial to President Obama's 2008 victory. Election night exit polls indicated that an estimated 67 percent of Hispanics voted for Obama, compared with 32 percent who voted for his Republican opponent, John McCain. That represented an eight percentage point improvement over 2004 when Democrat John Kerry garnered 59 percent of the Latino national vote to 40 percent for George W. Bush.

Part of this swing is attributable to the shrill GOP rhetoric against illegal immigration and in favor of strict border controls and workplace raids. Conservative Republicans have been especially vocal on security and enforcement issues, and some Hispanics perceived the party as hostile to Hispanic interests, including improving the situation for Hispanic immigrants.

In several states, Obama's share of the Hispanic vote exceeded his overall margin of electoral victory. For example, Obama carried Colorado by seven percentage points, while his share of the Hispanic vote was twelve percentage points higher than McCain's share. He won Florida by two points but had a nearly eight-point margin over McCain among Hispanics in the state. Obama recorded similar margins among Hispanic voters in Nevada and New Mexico.

Hispanics are also critical in competitive congressional races, especially in the South and West. Because they are clustered in key states and constitute a swing vote in several congressional districts, they have political influence disproportionate to their actual size. As Hispanics become more politically active and likely to vote, they are even more essential to successful electoral coalitions. By 2030 the U.S. Census Bureau estimates that Latinos will make up 20 percent of the American population. And in 2050 they will represent nearly one-quarter of all Americans.

This changing demographic alters the long-term political dynamic from earlier periods when reform efforts failed. Latinos' growing political power emboldens proponents to seek comprehensive legislation, while defusing potential opponents. The spread of Hispanics into suburban districts, where they previously had not been present, pressures legislators in each party to moderate their stances and respond to new local constituents. It remains to be seen whether these political and demographic shifts will be sufficient to persuade Congress to enact fundamental changes.

Shifts in Advocacy Group Positions

One feature that has doomed many earlier attempts to enact immigration reform has been an unwillingness on the part of key interest groups to compromise over key principles. Recently, however, some interest groups have indicated that they may be shifting their positions.

For example, labor unions historically have been lukewarm to immigration reform because some of their members perceive job competition from new arrivals. Especially when the economy has been weak, labor has focused more on protecting existing jobs than on recruiting new members. In 2009, however, two union federations, the AFL-CIO and Change to Win, announced a willingness to accept provisions that previously were anathema to each. In a formal declaration, each publicly announced that it would accept future increases in immigration, a key bone of contention in past discussions, if an independent immigration commission indexed temporary worker programs to economic conditions. Currently, Congress makes legislative decisions regarding the number of temporary workers, and its actions have not been well-calibrated to rising or falling employment. With this agreement, however, these federations expressed willingness to accept increases in short-term workers as long as labor market conditions are incorporated in future flow decisions.

This is exactly the type of interest group behavior that has been missing from past efforts at immigration reform. As long as each group holds to long-standing interests and principles, changes in immigration policy will prove elusive. Willingness to compromise represents a key sign of a shifting political landscape and an opportunity to implement reform. It does not guarantee actual legislation, but it does creates new potential for legislators to overcome intransigent group positions and take concrete action.

Of course, there remain interests that are unwilling to compromise. Immigration restrictionists whose opposition to reform stems from ethnocentrism or bigotry are intransigent. Others who cite economic interests, personal preferences, or policy principles for their opposition also will not be likely to compromise. Those who equate immigrant rights with civil rights will not want to sacrifice basic principles. An inability or unwillingness to negotiate remains an important barrier to policy change for many groups in this area.

THE NEED FOR NEW INSTITUTIONAL ARRANGEMENTS
TO OVERCOME PAROCHIALISM AND EMOTION

Despite the potential for legislation on immigration, the current institutional situation makes undertaking comprehensive reform on any issue problematic. The backlash against Obama's health care plan demonstrates how easy it is for opponents to block action by criticizing major policy changes as "too radical" or "too expensive."

Right now, jurisdiction over immigration policy is shared between four committees in both the House and Senate—Judiciary, Homeland Security, Agriculture, and Government Operations. These committees, some of which are highly polarized, have competing interests and different political dynamics, making it difficult to envision how members would deal with comprehensive change in the immigration area. Even if legislation were to reach the floor, individual legislators opposed to reform have the ability to block or delay action, particularly in the Senate. The decentralized structures, the polarized rhetoric, and the widespread citizen fear and anxiety surrounding immigration debate undermine the ability of elected politicians to engage in calm deliberations and make sound immigration decisions.

The persistent nature of these obstacles suggests it is time to alter institutional arrangements in a way that helps political leaders overcome their own history of parochialism and emotionalism. As pointed out earlier, political deliberations should focus on long-term national objectives, and institutional structures should insulate elected officials from having to make impossible political choices (such as the trade-off of admitting more extended family members versus high-skilled foreign workers). Because such decisions are "lose-lose" for elected officials, they are unlikely to be made.

On other controversial issues, Congress has opted for various types of institutional arrangements in which members set broad policy while administrative agencies work out the details.[36] For example, legislators generally do not develop technical requirements for radio and television broadcasters, preferring to leave that to the Federal Communications Commission. Similarly, regulation of the environment has devolved to the Environmental Protection Agency because of the complex, controversial, and technical nature of issues in that area. Rather than having legislators get involved in the minutiae of banks and other financial institutions, they are regulated by several federal agencies, including the Securities and Exchange Commission and the Federal Reserve.

Given the technical issues involved in immigration reform and the virtue of depoliticizing the conflict, some advocacy organizations have proposed the creation of a federal immigration commission with authority to make decisions within broad parameters enunciated by Congress. Such a commission would not resolve the issue of how to enact comprehensive immigration reform. But once broad principles are determined by legislators, having an independent agency gather unbiased data and implement specific decisions would help in the long run to reduce contentiousness surrounding immigration discussions.

For example, the Migration Policy Institute has proposed creation of a standing commission on immigration and labor markets that would reconcile the relationship between immigration, wages, and jobs.[37] Similar to the way the Social Security Commission operates, this group would draw on experts from a variety of political backgrounds and perspectives and seek to make reasonable decisions in the national interest.

Bill Galston of the Brookings Immigration Roundtable goes one step further. He and his colleagues suggest the creation of the equivalent of a Federal Reserve Bank system for immigration.[38] This body would have the power to make and implement technical adjustments in immigration flows depending on the state of the economy, labor flows, and national needs.

Still another variation on this theme is the development of an independent immigration commission. It would be similar to the Federal Communications Commission or Environmental Protection Agency in that it would be authorized to make immigration policy within broad confines outlined by Congress. Commissioners appointed by the president and confirmed by the Senate would set policy and determine the future course of immigration, independent of congressional political pressure.

Another approach is modeled on the procedure used for closing military bases. In this case, legislators have opted for an outside commission that recommends which bases should be mothballed. The commission collects information and periodically prepares a list of bases that are no longer needed. It then transmits these suggestions to Congress. Members can veto the entire list, but they cannot stop a particular base from being closed. This approach represents a mechanism for legislators to overcome their own parochialism. Because it is politically difficult for any lawmaker to support a base closing in his or her district, Congress opted for an institutional device that forces representatives to accept or reject the entire list, not bargain over specific military camps.

While these various proposals represent variations on a theme, the current running through each is depoliticization, insulating members from parochial political pressures, and reliance on experts to make public policy.[39] Given the nation's history of misguided decisions, overreactions, and political stalemate on immigration, it makes sense to consider new institutional arrangements for resolving contentious issues in the immigration area.

Of course, questions are likely to arise over who would appoint an independent commission, whether experts could be "captured" by industry or advocacy organizations, and whether Congress actually could agree to create such a body. Most federal agency commissioners are appointed by the president, subject to Senate confirmation, a process that provides input from a variety of different constituencies. While this appointment mechanism does not guarantee that commissioners will be evenhanded, it encourages greater impartiality than members of Congress are likely to display. Persuading Congress to create an independent commission might be difficult because many lawmakers are loathe to give up power over a subject that engages so many people on various sides of the subject. Delegation to an administrative agency or independent body sacrifices control and denies legislators some of their current authority. But emotional topics are risky for members of Congress. An independent body would help to insulate members from partisan cross fire and protect them from political dangers in the immigration area.

CHAPTER FOUR

PROBLEMATIC MEDIA COVERAGE

THE NEWS MEDIA AND OPINION writers have always played an important role in American politics. Because most people do not have direct, personal experience with specific policy issues, journalists serve as crucial intermediary gatekeepers, agenda setters, and problem definers. Through their role in filtering the political news and putting daily events into a particular narrative, reporters and editors, columnists, talk show hosts, bloggers, and other opinion leaders affect how Americans see specific political developments and what they think is important for the country as a whole. On occasion, a movie or television show can also move public opinion in one direction or another.

Whatever the medium, its impact often occurs through subtle or indirect mechanisms. For example, news coverage of minority groups that relies on stereotypes can activate preexisting negative attitudes, leading people to harsher assessments than otherwise would be the case. At other times, media effects occur by priming attitudes or affecting what people consider to be important.[1] For example, violent drug murders in Mexico may lead people to associate crime with Mexicans and then with Mexicans migrating to the United States.

Although many people think news gatherers and opinion leaders serve important news and political functions, not everyone sees their contributions in a positive light. As discussed later in this chapter, at various points in American history, news reporters and commentators have been condemned for being biased, superficial, jingoistic, sensationalist, or uninformative. During many periods and on many issues, coverage often was not very substantive, headlines were overblown and misleading, and news stories focused on trivial issues to the detriment of broader concerns. Critics worried that many segments of the media created more problems for American politics than they solved and that the media did little to advance the country's civic dialogue.[2]

Throughout much of American history, reporting on immigration issues has been biased.[3] A review of U.S. print and broadcast news coverage from 1995 to 2005 undertaken by Kamla Pande found that it was "twice as likely to stress the costs of immigration as the benefits."[4] News reporters typically focused on immigration's costs to taxpayers, illegals taking government benefits, or the high costs of border security, Pande found. Given this emphasis, it is no wonder public opinion tilts in a negative direction against new arrivals.

Most of the major newspaper articles covered in the study mentioned a specific nationality group, and in those stories, reporters were twice as likely to identify the Hispanic immigrants as Hispanics than they were to identify the ethnicity of other immigrants. Journalists routinely linked race and ethnicity to immigration in ways that could foster animosity toward ethnic groups. This conjoining of national origins to immigration adds an emotional element to public opinion and intensifies racial and ethnic conflict.

Some of America's worst decisions over the past two centuries regarding immigration policy have been preceded by inflamed media coverage portraying new arrivals as dirty, dangerous, or downright un-American.[5] People complain about the noisiness, partisanship, and superficial reporting by the contemporary media, but coverage in earlier times was often overtly racist and discriminatory, filled with negative stereotypes and highly emotional rhetoric.

A review of immigration coverage over the past century and a half demonstrates how prominent news reporting has been in shaping negative attitudes about immigrants and the value of immigration. Patterns of news coverage often have been unfair, sensationalistic, or uninformative. Reporters have played to unflattering narratives, making it difficult for native-born citizens to develop a more informed understanding of immigration policy.[6]

Of course, not all reporting or entertainment outlets tilt against immigration. A review of news accounts shows that immigrant "rags to riches" stories are common, and there are headlines such as "USA Just Wouldn't Work without Immigrant Labor." Some major newspapers such as the *New York Times* take an editorial stance that generally supports immigration reform. Movies and television programs also reflect both negative and positive images of immigration. Whereas some influential movies have painted immigrants as drug runners or violent criminals, others such as *My Big Fat Greek Wedding, The Joy Luck Club, Far and Away, Stand and Deliver,* and *The Visitor* are unabashedly pro-immigrant. But these positive assessments often are drowned out by more critical commentaries.

In this chapter I review coverage of immigrants from 1850 to the present day. In the nineteenth century, much of the newspaper coverage of Chinese immigrants was blatantly racist. The early twentieth-century reporting on Irish and Italian immigrant factory workers emphasized problems related to their language, clannishness, drinking, and Catholicism. Late twentieth-century portraits of Asian, African, and Latin American immigrants often focused on their racial, ethnic, and cultural differences from white Americans. And in the past decade, many talk radio and television hosts and programs have fanned the public's fears about legal and illegal immigrants sapping financial resources, contributing to crime and violence, and undermining American civic life.

Over the past century and a half, numerous stories have featured unfavorable "frames" or styles of coverage for immigrants. Currently, the narrative focuses on immigrants who enter the country illegally and take resources from native-born residents. Although no public opinion data exist for earlier time periods, it is likely that similar negative narratives inflamed public opinion and led government officials to make hasty, often short-sighted decisions rather than calmly debate policy alternatives and make sound policy choices.

What is needed today is a new reporting narrative that recognizes the "brain gain" America has received from immigration. As noted in the opening chapter, foreign newcomers have made many contributions to the country's economic, social, intellectual, and cultural life. When the United States takes border security more seriously and puts greater resources into stopping illegal immigration, the news media should acknowledge that policy shift and balance discussions of "illegality" with objective explanations of the impacts of enhanced security and the economic and intellectual benefits of new arrivals. That style of coverage would help Americans develop a more nuanced view of this important policy issue and lead to calmer and more reasonable public debates.[7]

NINETEENTH CENTURY REPORTING ON CHINESE IMMIGRANTS

Blatantly racist accounts of Chinese immigrants in news coverage and editorials probably contributed to the hostile public feelings about the Chinese during the nineteenth century (although it also is possible that negative public opinion encouraged journalists to write critical stories about those immigrants).

Following are several examples chosen from *Harper's Weekly,* which was by no means alone in its editorial animosity to Chinese immigrants (nor are these examples the only such stories *Harper's* carried during the twenty-year period). Referring to the Chinese, an 1857 article warned that "no one can disguise the dangers which environ the blending of hostile races into one people."[8] An 1860 *Harper's* story intoned, "It must always be remembered that Chinese ethics are not our ethics, and that a Chinaman considers it no wrong to cheat a party with whom he deals. This is true of Coolie porters, and of every class of Chinese, up to the highest court officials and the Emperor himself. To lie and to deceive are not crimes in the eye of Chinese morality."[9]

Five years later another *Harper's* story complained about Chinese students in San Francisco schools: "The pupils could not be brought to pay any attention to geography. They said, 'We believe the earth is level; but suppose it is round, what difference will it make to us? We won't make any more money whether it is round or square.' This indifference as to whether they make money on the square or not shows a low state of morality among the Chinese."[10]

In 1876 a *Harper's* story complained about the lack of entrepreneurship among the Chinese. "As merchants the Mongolians are not successful. They lack the reckless spirit of venture through which the Caucasian produces such fabulous results," the reporter wrote. "The whole secret of their success in laying up money lies in the fact that they are the stingiest and most parsimonious race on earth."[11] Instead of seeing high savings as a virtue, this reporter spun the characteristic in a negative direction.

Another *Harper's* story echoed this theme, writing that the Chinese are "content with quarters and fare at which a well-bred and respectable dog would turn up his nose."[12] The reporter not only failed to acknowledge that necessity forced new immigrants into low-paying positions and shoddy accommodations but also assumed that they had no higher aspirations. A reader might be forgiven for thinking that the foreigners had chosen to turn down well-paying jobs, more comfortable housing, and better food. In this style of coverage, *Harper's* reporting was typical of coverage throughout the United States that helped to shape the political climate of the times.

Another publication, the *Illustrated Wasp* in San Francisco, openly called for the Chinese to be expelled in 1878. "There are not a thousand people in California, outside of the Chinese themselves, who do not wish to see the last pigtail sail west through the Golden Gate," a reporter wrote. "When labor was scarce in California there might have been a shade of necessity for the employment of the Chinese; but now, when thousands of men and women are out of work, there is no good reason why the Celestials should be retained." The story ended by calling for "the removal of the Chinese curse."[13] That same year, the newspaper published a cartoon complaining that a severe famine in northwest China was likely to increase Chinese immigration to America. It depicted the possible immigrants as a "swarm of grasshoppers driven along by the inexorable hand of Famine." The *Wasp* said there still was time "to avert this danger" and avoid "our destruction as a nation."[14]

One of the fears about Chinese immigrants involved opium dens. An enduring theme of immigrant coverage is its focus on illegality and threats to the social order. Immigrants who use drugs and break laws are staples of this kind of coverage, and these kinds of descriptions of immigrant personal behavior—true for some immigrants—are then used to frame all new arrivals as undeserving and unworthy of American citizenship.

An *Illustrated Wasp* artist depicted several images of drug depravity in Chinatown arising from opium abuse. The artist drew images with captions such as "The King of the Opium Smokers," "Life and Death," "A Gambling House," and "Habitués of Chinatown." The images were accompanied by a news story describing the opium dens. After several hours touring squalid conditions, the reporter noted that "it was several days before the sickly fumes of this filthy blot on our modern civilization were fully dissipated from our minds."[15]

An April 16, 1892, *Harper's Weekly* editorial argued that "there is no question that the Chinese are the most undesirable of immigrants, because, with all their useful qualities, they cannot assimilate socially or politically or morally with Americans."[16] Another story that year in the *San Francisco Wave* complained about local press coverage of the Chinese. Following the disappearance of a young girl named Emma Wacker, Chinese were falsely accused and described as "moral and physical lepers" who "decoyed the child from her home, and . . . abused her fearfully. With diabolical ingenuity these brutalized heathens, or heathenized brutes . . . enticed the girl into their loathsome dens, and had foully wronged her."[17]

News coverage that frames immigrants as threatening social order and damaging the national character contributes to a political climate that encourages extreme policies and discriminatory actions. The Chinese often were characterized as standoffish, lazy, immoral, and dirty. This style of coverage laid the groundwork for the exclusionary policies that were adopted by local, state, and national authorities during the nineteenth century.

COVERAGE OF IRISH AND ITALIAN IMMIGRANTS IN THE EARLY 1900S

Harsh media coverage was not limited to the Chinese. Virtually every large immigration movement in American history has been accompanied by unfavorable media coverage of that particular group and unfriendly policy actions. The Chinese were one of the first objects of repressive immigration stories, but they hardly would be the last.

Much of the anti-immigration sentiment that emerged in the early twentieth century came from prominent opinion leaders whose views were carried in the newspapers or broadcast over the radio. Most of the vituperation was directed at the waves of Irish and Italian immigration that came to America between 1880 and 1920. Driven by famine and poor economic circumstances in Europe, more than 4.5 million Irish and 2.5 million Italians emigrated to the United States. Many of the Italians did not speak

English, and many Irish and Italians were Catholic, unlike most native-born Americans, who were Protestants.

Prominent opinion leaders railed against these new immigrants and their potential danger to the United States. One of these was Francis Walker, a highly quoted economist who gained fame for his attacks on laissez-faire economics and the development of modern economics, but who also argued vehemently on behalf of "protecting the American rate of wages, the American standard of living, and the quality of American citizenship from degradation through the tumultuous access of vast throngs of ignorant and brutalized peasantry from the countries of eastern and southern Europe."[18] From his standpoint, America needed strict limits on immigration to protect its culture and economy from the new arrivals. Foreigners added little to American life because of their lack of education, he said, and the United States needed to keep out these "peasants" if it wanted to keep its living standard high and its civic life pure.

Warning even more directly about the racial aspects of immigration was commentator William Ripley. He complained about European people who "have dropped from the sky. They are in the land, but not yet an integral part of it. The population product is artificial and exotic." Employing evolutionary reasoning in his critique, he worried about the flood of European immigrants to the United States and "the radical change in its character, in the source from whence it comes."[19]

Even a progressive socialist writer such as Randolph Bourne worried that immigrants to America would bring their "belligerent, exclusive, inbreeding, the poison of which we are witnessing now in Europe." In his writings for the *New Republic* and other magazines, he was vehemently opposed to World War I. Bourne described the "failure of the 'melting-pot'" and the "failure of Americanization." Rather than becoming another Europe that was divided and balkanized, he wanted the United States to "liberate and harmonize the creative power of all these peoples and give them the new spiritual citizenship."[20] If immigrants became assimilated Americans, they would be far less corrosive to the national culture.

Social commentator Don Lescohier complained about immigrants from Europe and Asia. Writing of the "radical socialistic movements shaking Europe to-day," he said that European immigrants had radical political views that would be very dangerous for the United States. He also warned that the "effort to reopen our gates to Oriental immigration is nothing less than suicidal." If Asians came to America, he argued, they would "develop a hatred of our economic system, and even of our government," and thus would also endanger the United States. He concluded his article by urging that immigration be stopped for ten years, a proposal he said would not harm America's industrial development but would have positive benefits for the country.[21]

Not surprising, given the tone of this commentary, many Americans at the time had unfavorable views of the new wave of immigration sweeping across the continent. Anti-immigrant editorials were backed up by jingoistic reporting in much of the press harping on alleged shortcomings of the Irish and Italians. Some newspapers carried classified job postings stipulating, in boldface capital letters, that NO IRISH NEED APPLY.[22] When 650 "Irish paupers" arrived in Boston, a *Harper's Weekly* cartoon complained that "the balance of trade with Great Britain seems to be still against us." To reinforce this sharp point regarding "low-end" arrivals, the picture of the Irish transport boat in the newspaper cartoon showed a group of Irishmen labeled "Poor House from Galway."[23]

Another magazine cartoon warned of "lazy Irish" who "wait for money," compared with native-born Americans who are "working for it."[24] A *Puck* cartoon noted that "the raw Irishman in America is a nuisance, his son a curse. They never assimilate; the second generation simply shows an intensification of all the bad qualities of the first. . . .They are a burden and a misery to this country."[25] These cartoons reflected the widely held sentiment that these new arrivals were more trouble than they were worth.

Another *Harper's Weekly* cartoon warned about the dangers for American schools. According to the cartoonist, "Public schools are threatened by Catholicism; and American children are forced to worship at strange altars."[26] The clear message was that if too many Catholic immigrants were allowed in the country, freedom of religion would be in danger.

Others worried about detrimental ramifications for national civic life. One illustrator showed Lady Liberty dressed in the American flag attempting to mix immigrants into a bowl called Citizenship. However, this concoction never solidified, according to this illustrator because "the Irish is unmixable in the national pot."[27]

In 1883 Emma Lazarus wrote the now-famous welcoming creed "Give me your tired, your poor, your huddled masses yearning to breathe free," words that were later engraved on the Statue of Liberty. Her poem reflected her belief that America was an immigrant nation that took in the poor, gave them economic opportunities, and benefited from their resulting hard work and creativity. Yet those who embraced Lazarus's view of immigrant contributions to American life found it hard, amid the outpouring of negative news stories, editorials, cartoons, and commentary, to defuse the hostile public and leadership opinion that was so common during the late 1800s and early 1900s.

In 1924 Congress put sharp brakes on immigration policy by slapping "national origins quotas" on immigrants from specific nations. Immigration was limited to 2 percent of the number of people from that nation living in the United States in 1890. It barred outright immigration from a number of Asian countries, including China, Japan, Korea, Singapore, and the Philippines. Immigration levels fell almost immediately and remained low for the next four decades, restricted not only by legislated limits but also by the Great Depression and World War II.

COVERAGE OF MINORITY IMMIGRANTS IN THE LATE 1900S

Hostile immigration rules more or less remained in effect until 1965, when the country reopened its borders and allowed more newcomers to move to America. Twenty years after winning World War II, there was widespread public recognition that the U.S. victory had been enormously aided by immigrants whose scientific theories and technological innovations had led to the first atomic bomb and other significant developments. In the economic prosperity that followed the war, Americans felt more confident about their place in the world and became more welcoming of immigrants. The 1965 Celler-Hart legislation eliminated national quotas and allowed more people to qualify for American visa programs. As a result, the number and diversity of immigrants coming into the country increased.

It did not take long, however, for the flood of new arrivals to stimulate another round of public and media backlash against immigration. Even though President Johnson and leading senators sought to reassure a concerned public that the 1965 law would not affect their lives or the number or ethnic mix of immigrants, the truth proved otherwise.

The late 1900s saw new fears about immigrants coming from Cuba, Haiti, and Mexico, among other places. Unlike the situation with the Irish and Italians, who shared America's predominantly European ancestry, the new arrivals differed in race, ethnicity, culture, education, and job skills.[28] This wave of minority immigration generated negative reactions from many Americans.

The Carter administration welcomed a flood of Cuban arrivals through the Mariel boatlift with what the president called "open heart and open arms." Between April and September 1980, 120,000 Cubans came to America. Refugee camps were set up at military bases in Arkansas, Pennsylvania, and Wisconsin. Unlike the upper class and professional Cuban immigrants of earlier

years, however, many of the new arrivals were poor and unedu-
cated. Neither the immigrants nor native-born Americans were
very happy about the situation. Food and housing proved to be
enormous problems. Riots at one camp resulted in injuries to
forty-two Cubans and sixteen camp officials. In August 1980
Cuban refugees disillusioned with their new life in America were
involved in six airplane hijackings in efforts to go home.[29]

Press coverage debated whether the new guests were "delin-
quents, bums, parasites, and drug addicts," as alleged by Cuban
president Fidel Castro, or a "cross-section of Cuban society" that
included doctors, workers, farmers, and artists.[30] One *Time* magazine story described Florida as "Trouble in Paradise" and noted
that an "epidemic of violent crime, a plague of illicit drugs and
a tidal wave of refugees have slammed into South Florida with
the destructive power of a hurricane. . . . The wave of illegal
immigrants has pushed up unemployment, taxed social services,
irritated racial tensions and helped send the crime rate to stagger-
ing heights. Marielitos are believed to be responsible for half of
all violent crime in Miami." Others praised Cuban immigrants for
being anticommunist and vehement in their opposition to Castro
The problematic coverage led Miami Mayor Maurice Ferre to
conclude, "We've become a boiling pot, not a melting pot."[31]
Public discontent rose to the point where South Florida bumper
stickers plaintively noted, "Will the Last American Leaving South
Florida Please Bring the Flag."[32]

Similar controversies plagued new arrivals from Haiti. A 1992
Time magazine story voiced the unequivocal title of "Send 'Em
Back!" to convey the message that Haitians were not welcome in
the United States and that the public was angry about the Haitian
immigration wave.[33] Another *Time* article was entitled "Opening
the Border to AIDS." It focused on 200 Haitians seeking to enter
the United States who had tested positive for AIDS. Under U.S.
policy, individuals testing positive for syphilis, AIDS, gonorrhea,
leprosy, or tuberculosis could be denied entry to the United States.

Representative Tom DeLay (R-Texas) explained, "You don't open your gates when you're trying to control a disease within your borders." The story cited government estimates of $100,000 to treat the typical AIDS patient from "diagnosis to death."[34]

Indeed, much like the situation that developed with Chinese in the 1800s, this fusing of illegal immigration and deadly disease became a common storyline.[35] The *New American* published a story in 2006 titled "A Resurgence of Deadly Diseases," claiming that illegal immigrants were responsible for a resurgence of leprosy and tuberculosis in the United States, diseases once thought to have been eradicated. "Illegal immigrants carry loathsome diseases for which American medicine is ill-prepared," the reporter wrote.[36] Although no evidence was presented to back up this incendiary claim, it fit the popular narrative that illegal immigrants were unhealthy and therefore dangerous for America. When the swine flu emerged in Mexico and spread across the United States in 2009, the National Association of Hispanic Journalists issued a press release urging the news media to "resist baseless blame of immigrants as it covers a possible pandemic." The association's board of directors worried that Mexican immigrants would become "scapegoats" for the outbreak. "We have come to expect immigrant bashing from the usual suspects—commentators who use purposefully inflammatory rhetoric to seek attention and to suit their agenda. And they haven't disappointed, now using the swine flu as cause to decry immigration and immigrants," the release said.[37]

Overall press coverage of Mexican immigrants has been little more positive. Elvira Arellano became a symbol in 2006 as an illegal immigrant working at Chicago's O'Hare Airport, where she was caught and prosecuted for using a forged Social Security number.[38] Facing deportation, she took sanctuary in a church for a year but then was arrested and sent back to Mexico when she attempted to move to Los Angeles with her eight-year-old child. Arellano provoked outrage when she compared herself to activist

Rosa Parks, whose refusal to move to the back of a city bus in defiance of segregation laws helped spark the civil rights movement of the 1950s and 1960s. "I'm strong, I've learned from Rosa Parks—I'm not going to the back of the bus. The law is wrong," Arellano complained.

Critics across the United States went ballistic over this analogy. Numerous writers and commentators pointed out that, in drawing this comparison, she revealed her ignorance about the history of American slavery and that hardships American minorities had to overcome. One columnist described Arellano as merely "pimping the system" and not understanding that she had violated the law in coming to the United States illegally.[39]

But no case drew the avalanche of media and public attention as did that of Elian Gonzales in 2000. The young boy was a passenger in a boat filled with people fleeing from Cuba. The boat capsized near the Florida coast, drowning Elian's mother and several others. Elian was rescued and turned over to relatives in Miami, touching off a custody battle between his Cuban father and the Florida relatives that garnered not only national but international news coverage.

The Immigration and Naturalization Service (INS) ruled that the boy should be returned to his Cuban father, a decision backed by the attorney general, Janet Reno. In keeping with internationally accepted law that children should be reunited with parents whenever possible, the Clinton administration agreed that Elian should be returned to Cuba despite his dramatic voyage to the United States and the emotional pleas of his American family that he not be sent back to a poor and authoritarian country. But it took an armed INS raid to wrest the boy from his relatives' home and reunite him with his father back in Cuba. As television cameras recorded the tense scene, government agents grabbed the crying young boy and carried him to a waiting van. He was then flown to Andrews Air Force Base, where he was reunited with his father, who had come to the United States to pick Elian up, and the two then returned to Cuba.

Media reporting of the episode emphasized several competing perspectives. One narrative centered on the trauma of the family dispute, the young mother who died at sea, the Miami relatives who wanted to keep the boy in America, and the Cuban father who demanded and won repatriation of his son. Another contrasted the case of Cuban versus Haitian émigrés and what Haitians argued was overly favorable treatment of Cuban arrivals. Still another storyline focused on the immigration raid by armed agents and the personal trauma inflicted on the Gonzales family by the government action. Together the stories about the case illustrated the various crosscurrents in views regarding illegal immigrants in the United States.[40]

Differential coverage of Cubans and Haitians was documented in a study undertaken by Manoucheka Celeste. She examined *New York Times* articles about the two groups from 1994 through 2004. Although she found that both ethnic groups were framed negatively, Cubans were covered more positively than Haitians. She found 70 positive and 78 negative frames for Cubans, compared with 23 positive and 206 negative frames about Haitians. The latter were portrayed as being poor, living in a troubled nation, having character weaknesses, and being primitive.[41] Little in these news stories would encourage Americans to welcome Haitians newly arrived in the United States.

THE NEW MEDIA ENVIRONMENT:
TALK RADIO, BLOGS, AND SOCIAL MEDIA

In recent years a declining economy has placed enormous fiscal pressures on news organizations all around the globe. The simultaneous declines in ad revenues and circulation levels have undermined the traditional business model of newspapers, radio, and television. Virtually every trend in traditional print readership, viewership, and ad revenues is down and not likely to get better any time soon. Daily print circulation has declined from 62 million to 49 million nationwide over the last twenty years. Readership for leading newspapers such as the *New York Times* is down 10 percent just in the past two years alone.[42]

Advertising revenue at many papers has dropped by 25 percent since 2006. Newspapers such as the *Rocky Mountain News, Seattle Post-Intelligencer, Ann Arbor News,* and *Tucson Citizen* have closed for good, while others such as the *Chicago Tribune, Minneapolis Star Tribune,* and *Philadelphia Inquirer* went into bankruptcy in 2009 and had to be restructured.[43] Layoffs are occurring at many media outlets across the land. The *Los Angeles Times* has gone from a news staff of 1,200 to 600 in the past decade.

Readership problems are not unique to these outlets. ABC television's D.C. staffing dropped from 46 people in 1985 to 15 in 2008, and the network recently announced that it was laying off 300 or more newsroom workers overall. CBS recently laid off more than 100 newsroom employees. In the print area, the number of newspapers with D.C. bureaus dropped from over 600 in 1985 to 300 in 2008, and more have closed since. Newhouse newspapers, Cox newspapers, Copley News Service, the *Los Angeles Times, Chicago Tribune, Baltimore Sun,* and *Hartford Courant* closed their Washington bureaus. The *Washington Post* recently merged its business section with the rest of the paper and closed most of its U.S. bureaus. Some newspapers such as the *Christian Science Monitor* have given up on print and migrated entirely to the web.[44] National Public Radio is alone among traditional media, with its listener audience rising 9 percent in 2008 over the preceding year.[45]

At the same time that media finances have imploded, the popularity of the Internet has led many people to forsake traditional print and broadcast information for free online content. Nielsen Online estimates that 75 million Americans read papers online.

For the first time in history, that number is higher than the comparable figure for print sources.

One of the most noteworthy features of the new media system is the democratization of news gathering.[46] In the old regime, professional journalists served as the primary gatekeepers. They gathered the news, placed information in context, and decided what was important. Today, however, news gathering is more democratic because it involves a broader range of people serving as news gatherers, commentators, and interpreters of political events.[47] Although many of these news gatherers do little more than offer their own personal opinion with no independent reporting, they help shape the media milieu in which people form opinions.

Citizen journalism takes a variety of different forms: instant news reporting from ordinary citizens, crisis coverage from eyewitnesses on the scene, and blogging and commentary. CNN has "I-Reporters" who upload video reporting, commentary, or analysis to the network. Meanwhile, Current TV specializes in "viewer-provided content," which consists of news or entertainment features from viewers around the world. Some citizens even upload pictures and videos directly to news organizations. During recent student protests in Iran, participants blogged and tweeted about events taking place on the streets and therefore provided the only source of information for people who were not there.[48]

Bloggers provide commentary on virtually every political and public policy topic. For example, it is estimated that more than 5,000 blogs in the United States are devoted to the topic of education. There are blogs for current college students, activists seeking school reform, technology advocates, high school students who exchange salacious gossip about their fellow pupils, and professors and teachers who express their views through digital platforms.

During times of crises, disasters, and emergencies when professional journalists are not yet on the scene, these new outlets allow eyewitnesses to inform the public about what is happening. They provide timely and relevant information that supplements the work of trained reporters. With new digital technologies, the news industry is more democratic and interactive than ever before, drawing on a broad range of amateur and professional practitioners.

However, the free-wheeling atmosphere of this new media universe has complicated civic discussions surrounding emotional policy issues such as immigration. Currently, representatives of the new media tend be opinionated, highly personalized, and apt to inflame passions on all sides of controversial issues. The contemporary media are noisy and polarizing, making it harder for citizens to obtain objective information about policy controversies.[49]

Witness the shocking rhetoric of Boston radio talk show host Jay Severin. During public worry over the spread of swine flu from Mexico, he derided Mexicans as "leeches," "the world's lowest of primitives," and the home of "women with mustaches and VD." These comments got him suspended, but not fired, by station WTKK-FM.[50] Although his remarks might have been the most intemperate, Severin was not alone in his sentiments. Conservative radio host Michael Savage complained about illegal aliens being "carriers of the new strain of human-swine avian flu from Mexico" and demanded that the U.S.-Mexican border be "closed immediately."[51]

Divisive new media coverage was a major roadblock to Senate passage of comprehensive immigration reform in 2007. According to a Brookings study undertaken by Roberto Suro, traditional news reporting "played a very direct role in heightening the polarization on immigration issues." The dominant narrative of print writers centered on "illegality," which contributed to negative public perceptions about immigration.

News coverage of immigration issues increased in 2006 and 2007 but still trailed coverage of other major issues. In 2007, for example, nearly 10.8 percent of news reports focused on the

2008 election campaign, compared with 7.8 percent focused on Iraq policy, 5.9 percent on events in Iraq , 2.9 percent on immigration, 2.4 percent on Iran, and 2 percent on domestic terrorism. According to Suro, conservative talk show hosts, who are typically opposed to immigration, gave immigration four times as much attention as did liberal hosts. That helps to explain why negative public attitudes toward immigration hardened.

Talk shows represented a particular influential venue for discussion during the 2006–07 congressional debate over immigration reform. The mainstream media devoted 9.2 percent of its overall coverage in early 2007 to immigration, compared with 22 percent for talk radio and 43.1 percent for then CNN television host Lou Dobbs.[52] Using the vehicle of his evening show on CNN, Dobbs night after night castigated undocumented aliens as an "army of invaders" who deliberately had what he called "anchor babies" in the United States to keep themselves from being deported.[53]

Writer E. J. Dionne analyzed the "Dobbs effect" on attitudes toward immigration policy. It should be noted that complex methodological issues are involved in attributing public opinion impact to particular television outlets. For example, people who watch Dobbs or other conservative critics may already be more hostile to immigrants or foreigners. This kind of "self-selection" makes it difficult to know what impact is attributable to the media show versus the views of the audience itself.

However, Dionne's analysis of a Pew Research Center national public opinion survey shows little evidence of audience self-selection. Overall, there were few differences in attitudes between Dobbs' viewers and nonviewers. Fifty-three percent of those listening regularly to Dobbs favored providing a way for illegal immigrants to gain legal citizenship if they passed background checks, paid fines, and had jobs, compared with 55 percent who did not listen to him. But the differences were greater among those holding conservative-to-moderate viewpoints. Among this group, 43 percent of listeners favored a pathway to citizenship, compared with 59 percent of nonlisteners. This group also tended to be the segment most opposed to Congress enacting a comprehensive solution to immigration.[54]

Based on this analysis, Dionne concluded that "talk radio accelerated the movement of Republicans away from compromise. Lou Dobbs' efforts raised the price of compromise for Democrats. And taken together, talk radio and Dobbs were by far the most energetic and opinionated voices in the immigration debate."[55] This impact differed considerably from the mainstream media. According to Dionne, "The traditional media lacked the interest in the issue shown by passionate media opponents of immigration reform, and the more liberal media were far less engaged in the issue than their conservative counterparts."[56]

Bloggers, Internet websites, and social media clearly have diversified coverage of immigration issues. Voices vary across the media landscape depending on point of view and personal experience.[57] There are more outlets than ever before because the barriers to entry into the reporting area are quite low. Virtually any one can set up a website, write a blog, or become a CNN I-reporter.

But the resulting media cacophony has further undermined the ability of political leaders to discuss immigration in a rational and civil manner. In the highly polarized world of new media, compromise often has become a dirty word. New media outlets play to public prejudice by presenting distinctly unflattering views of new arrivals. In such a charged atmosphere, politicians are less likely to be able to resolve conflicts and reach legislative compromises.[58]

A NEW STYLE OF IMMIGRATION COVERAGE

Media coverage in recent years has emphasized a narrative of illegality and high costs associated with immigration.[59] But coverage of immigrants does not have to be so unfair, biased, and one-sided. Food sections of major newspapers are filled with stories about the culinary variety added to American life though foreign cuisines. Readers do not necessarily associate the widespread availability of ethnic food in the United States with immigration even though many restaurants featuring global cuisine are owned and operated by immigrants. This is just one of the ways journalists could help people understand immigrant contributions to American life and defuse controversies surrounding immigration.

Another way is to focus on high-skilled scientists and engineers. Many of the new technology firms that have blossomed in recent decades were founded by recent immigrants.[60] Often, these were individuals educated in the United States who were then hired by American businesses and later formed their own business companies. These enterprises have fueled innovation in the United States, improved productivity, and added greatly to the country's economic development.

The entrepreneurial spirit represented by these individuals is one reason the American economy has done well over the past few decades. These immigrant entrepreneurs brought new skills and extensive creativity to the country and helped create many jobs. Business magazines often profile Sergey Brin, Andrew Grove, Jerry Yang, and Pierre Omidyar as exemplars of American ingenuity, but they do not make the tie to public policies that allowed them to come to the United States for education and employment. Their successes are attributed to individual virtue, not to immigration policies that bring young talent to America for training and development.

Reporters need to draw the connection between immigration policies and long-term economic development. It is no accident that the United States became one of the global epicenters of the technology revolution. The combination of a higher education system that encouraged foreign students to come to the United States, a business sector that rewarded entrepreneurship, and government policies that allowed some talented foreigners to obtain employment visas helped fuel a technology boom that produced jobs and economic prosperity for the country as a whole.

While illegal immigration certainly warrants media attention as well as a government that takes border security seriously, news reporting that focuses heavily on illegality misses coverage of the brain gain that benefits the entire country. Some balance in this coverage would be more honest and would undermine the negative and erroneous public stereotypes that so inflame civic dialogue on immigration.[61]

It is not easy to know how to lead reporters to this style of coverage. In a fragmented and niche-oriented world, media outlets have advertising and marketing incentives to play to the base and emphasize coverage of interest to narrow slices of Americans. The current political economy of news gathering encourages reporters to emphasize conflict and sensationalize news stories, even if these articles exaggerate the overall costs of immigration. Harsh assessments inflame public sentiment but sometimes appear to sell more papers and attract more viewers than calmer and dispassionate interpretations.[62]

With the growing size and political importance of Hispanic and Asian voters, however, journalists and news organizations should realize that these ethnic groups represent a crucial niche and valuable source of ad dollars. Offending ethnic readers and viewers with biased, anti-immigrant coverage is not a sound long-term strategy on the part of news organizations.[63] It makes more sense to provide Latinos and Asians with coverage that recognizes the contributions they make to the United States and appeals to a population other than angry white males.[64] That approach would enable news and other media to reach a broader audience than currently is the case today as well as to appeal to a growing demographic in the media marketplace.

CHAPTER FIVE

SHIFTING PUBLIC OPINION

EMOTION IS NOT A NEW feature in American politics.[1] At various times in U.S. history, citizen resentments have built to such a pitch that voters have forced action on certain issues. For example, anger over high property taxes in California led to the 1978 Proposition 13 revolt, where voters imposed tough restrictions on future state tax hikes.[2] More recently, national attention has been focused on citizen "tea parties" protesting federal government proposals for health care, government spending, and failure to deal with high budget deficits.

Sometimes, anxiety has arisen about particular racial or ethnic groups.[3] Vigilante violence during the Reconstruction era was directed primarily at newly freed African American slaves. The Know-Nothings, active in the 1840s and 1850s, believed immigrants and Roman Catholics presented a threat to American values. At one time or another, the Irish, the Italians, eastern Europeans, Latin Americans, Africans, and Asians have all been perceived as posing some sort of threat to the American way of life. During the cold war, worry about the loyalty of communists and other radicals sparked repressive legislation and security crackdowns.[4]

Media coverage often amplifies negative citizen concerns about various groups.[5] Press attention to particular "threats" can elevate people's fears and lead them to single out those groups for harsh treatment. If public opposition is loud enough and persistent enough, politicians take notice, often passing legislation that imposes strict rules on the target population.[6]

According to historians and trend analysts, American public opinion tends to go through various public moods or policy cycles that mark the era and shape how officials deal in general with policy problems. [7] The plight of millions of jobless Americans during the Great Depression of the 1930s, for example, initiated a period of government intervention and regulation quite different from the more limited public sphere activities of early eras. Since 1980, when Ronald Reagan's calls for smaller government helped elect him president, public opinion has shifted once again, toward resistance to paying taxes and a more restricted conception of government actions.[8]

The public mood is important at these times because citizen views, policy streams, and leadership actions coincide to focus on particular problems.[9] The "culprit" in the policy area is defined in specific terms, and certain approaches become legitimized or delegitimized. The "villain" may be Catholics, immigrants, minorities, big business, labor unions, or government officials. Whatever the particular target, resentments build up over real or alleged deficiencies, and people mobilize to address those culprits and villains. The suggested "solutions" can have dramatic ramifications for the way government officials respond to specific issues.

Historically, American views on immigration have been especially complex and volatile and dependent on the particular political context.[10] The public often has developed xenophobic or emotional responses that compromise rational policymaking. These public sentiments have affected national deliberations and colored the overall shape of American immigration policy.[11]

In this chapter, I analyze changing public views about immigration. Public opinion on immigration issues has varied depending on the economy and political events. There are nuances in public opinion depending on country of origin, particular kinds of policy actions, and suggested policy remedies. Americans are more supportive of immigration from European countries than from Latin American, African, or Arabic nations. Public opinion surveys reveal that a majority of the public tends to support access to public education for immigrants but to oppose giving immigrants access to government-financed health care. Recent polls show that a majority of people favor an official "pathway to citizenship" for illegal immigrants currently in the United States *if* those here without visas learn English, have lived in the country for at least five years, have jobs, and pay a fine. The inflow of illegal people to the United States is at a thirty-year low, a fact that has reduced opposition to new legal arrivals and put the country in a position where it can contemplate significant policy changes.[12]

But politicians remain wary of policymaking in this area because public opinion can shift quickly. Data demonstrate that even though the issue does not rank highly as an overall national priority, it does have a significant effect on people's voting behavior. A relatively high percentage of Americans rate immigration as one of the most important factors affecting the way they judge politicians. Such attitudes, coupled with the general public's cynicism regarding the ability of the government to safeguard U.S. borders and to enforce laws barring employment of illegal immigrants, help explain why immigration remains a challenging issue for elected officials to address.[13]

ANGER AND ANXIETY IN AMERICAN POLITICS

Citizen anger and anxiety have played a role in American politics from the very beginning.[14] One of the earliest examples of public emotion came during revolutionary times in the form of the Boston Tea Party. Colonial complaints over British rule rose when the royal authorities adopted the Townshend Revenue Act of 1767 and the Tea Act of 1773. Designed to raise revenue for the British government, both acts imposed a tax on tea delivered to the colonies.

A vigilante group known as the Sons of Liberty formed to oppose the tea tax. Not only did colonists object to the tax on a popular beverage but they also objected to being taxed by the British government when North America had no elected representatives in Parliament, arguing that such "taxation without representation" compromised their colonial rights.[15]

The protests centered on Boston because it was the largest tea-importing city in North America. Similar protests had arisen in New York, Philadelphia, and Charleston, but those crises were averted when British authorities returned the tea ships to England without unloading the cargo. Boston was the lone exception to this maneuver—the king's representative in Boston, Governor Thomas Hutchinson, confronted the protesters and refused to allow the boats to return without the tea tax being paid.

Samuel Adams organized a series of meetings of thousands of area residents to protest Hutchinson's intransigence. Over a period of several weeks, the two sides were unable to reach agreement. On the night of December 16, 1773, colonial men boarded the tea ships *Dartmouth, Beaver,* and *Eleanor* anchored in Boston Harbor and emptied 342 chests of tea worth around 90,000 British pounds into the water. The act of insurrection incensed the British and sharply escalated the tensions between the royal government and the colonials, which soon led to the Revolutionary War and the colonies' declaration of independence from Great Britain.

The Boston Tea Party was not the only protest mounted by citizens angry with their government in colonial times. Daniel Shays led an armed insurrection in 1786 and 1787 protesting tax and debt burdens. Poor farmers in western Massachusetts unable to pay their debts were losing their farms to foreclosures and being sent to debtors' prisons. After petitioning the state legislature for help, several thousand men took up arms to prevent courts from taking land for unpaid debt. It took a militia organized by the Massachusetts Legislature to put down this local force.[16]

In the late 1800s vigilante violence during the Reconstruction period was directed at newly freed slaves who sought economic and political freedom.[17] Local rebels, mostly in southern and border states, used violence, lynchings, imprisonment, and beatings to intimidate African Americans into submission and poverty. In the years immediately following the end of the Civil War, African Americans had been elected to public office in record numbers. They won seats in every state legislature in the South, even gaining a majority in the lower chamber of the South Carolina legislature. In Mississippi the lieutenant governor, secretary of state, superintendent of education, and Speaker of the House were all black. Fourteen blacks were elected to the U.S. House of Representatives, and two served in the U.S. Senate.[18] On the surface, Reconstruction appeared to have extraordinary success in ending slavery and ushering in an era of social and political equality.

These gains, however, did not last. Following the contested presidential election of 1876, home rule was restored to the South in 1877, and federal troops stationed in the former Confederate states since the Civil War to maintain peace, were withdrawn.[19] White vigilante groups arose in every southern state. Beatings, threats, and harassment were employed to cow African Americans into submission.[20] From 1882 to 1930 an estimated 2,805 victims were lynched in ten southern states. Black voter turnout plummeted, and most black elected officials were turned out of office. By the end of the nineteenth century, blacks had been reduced to economic and political impoverishment.

The Great Depression of the 1930s provoked a series of protests arising from the dismal economic situation. With unemployment reaching above 25 percent, poverty and homelessness were widespread; many people found themselves living in shanty towns, known as Hoovervilles; and many suffered from inadequate food and health care.[21] Others had to rely on family and friends for basic necessities.

The widespread poverty and joblessness led to marches on Washington and protests directed at political leaders. Protesters complained that the government was not doing enough to help the poor and that Wall Street financiers were profiting from the nation's economic woes. Populist leaders such as Louisiana governor Huey Long used inflammatory rhetoric to push for policies that would redistribute wealth in the United States, proclaiming the need for a "chicken in every pot."[22] Father Charles E. Coughlin was another fomenter of emotional response to the Great Depression and government policies of that era.

During the late 1960s and early 1970s, Vietnam war protests eventually led members of Congress to cut funding for the war. Young people and other individuals unhappy over the course of that conflict held rallies and mass demonstrations designed to express discontent and get leaders to pull American troops out of that Southeastern Asian nation. In 1974 the United States withdrew from Vietnam.

In 1978 public concern over high local property taxes led to a tax revolt that has had a lingering effect on state and local government budgets. Disgruntled with a series of state tax increases, Californians used the state initiative process to gather signatures and place a measure, known as Proposition 13, on the ballot mandating limits on property tax increases. Two-thirds of the state's voters supported the measure, which cut property taxes by one-third and mandated that property taxes could increase by no more than 2 percent each fiscal year unless the property were sold.[23]

The passage of the California ballot measure led several other states and cities to enact their own tax limits. Twenty-four states have a ballot initiative process that allows voters to place issues directly before citizens, and in many of these states voters put antitax measures on the ballot. According to researcher Bill Piper, in the two decades following passage of Proposition 13, forty-one of the eighty-six antitax items on the ballot of various states were approved by voters.[24]

Most recently, angry Americans, stirred up by equally angry talk show hosts, have staged contemporary "tea parties" to protest rising federal debt, health care reform, and lack of fiscal moderation. Some use TEA as an acronym for "Taxed Enough Already." These events have protested "big government" and what some view as a dramatic expansion in public sector regulation and intervention.[25] Tens of thousands of people have shown up in 750 cities around the country to denounce current tax and spending policies. Not only have these events become a fulcrum of citizen outrage, they have attracted considerable media attention in the process. One apparent result of these intense sentiments has been a drop in public support for President Barack Obama and for health care reform, his signature domestic legislative priority.

EMOTIONS SURROUNDING IMMIGRATION

As with other controversial issues, anger is an important ingredient driving the public debate about immigration. Research by Ted Brader, Nicholas Valentino, and Elizabeth Suhay demonstrates that a sense of "group threat" triggers much of the anxiety and anger about immigrants. Residents worry that more generous entry policies will result in harm to themselves and to members of their racial or ethnic group. People who feel this way are less sympathetic to immigration and more likely to want to reduce the number of new arrivals.[26]

Antoine Banks found a similar dynamic in regard to white racial hostility to Hispanics. Using a public opinion survey, he found that anger triggered hostility and that angry people believed that minorities did not deserve to be the beneficiaries of immigration or affirmative action policies. Such beliefs, he found, undermined public support for immigration policy and made it more difficult for leaders to resolve controversies in these policy areas.[27]

In recent years, up to one-third of Americans have said they are angry about illegal immigration, while another third indicate they are frustrated that the government has not done more to stop unauthorized flows across the border. Most (83 percent) direct their anger at the government rather than at the immigrants themselves (12 percent).[28]

A majority of Americans say they understand why individuals from poor countries want to come to the United States. Given the relatively high standard of living and the economic opportunities, America is a huge magnet for many who are oppressed at home and who lack opportunities to make something of their own lives.[29]

But while Americans many understand what motivates immigrants to come to the United States, many are unsympathetic to what they perceive as the refusal of many immigrants to adopt American ways. Many Americans also blame government officials for this failure to assimilate. According to a recent national survey, 43 percent of Americans believe officials "encourage immigrants to retain the culture of their home country," while 32 percent disagree. Those who say they are angry about immigrants are much more likely to think that officials do not encourage immigrants to assimilate. Fifty-nine percent of individuals complain that officials allow immigrants to retain their original national culture despite being here. Seventy-seven percent of Americans say that those who come to the United States should adopt American culture.[30]

California's 1994 passage of Proposition 187, an anti-immigration initiative, demonstrates the depth of voter resentment. The ballot measure, designed to restrict immigrant access to health and education services, was approved by voters on a 59 to 41 percent margin. However, the proposition never took effect because a federal judge later ruled that the measure was discriminatory and therefore unconstitutional.[31]

An analysis of state polling data indicates that economic views were important to how people voted. Those with improving financial circumstances were more likely to support Proposition 187 than those who were poorer or whose prospects were not very bright.[32]

But a journalist also found a deeper cultural antagonism at the root of voter unhappiness with immigrant rights. Speaking to the *Economist,* one voter explained that use of the Mexican flag during campaign rallies was problematic. "The biggest mistake the opposition made was waving those green-and-white flags with the snake on them," this person announced. "They should have been waving the American flag."[33]

ECONOMIC SELF-INTEREST VERSUS RACIAL PREJUDICE

Different schools of thought offer different explanations for white opposition to immigration. One perspective centers on economic self-interest, positing that whites fear that new arrivals take jobs, reduce wages, evade taxes, and draw unfairly on government and social services. In other words, people define costs and benefits in economic terms, and many believe that the material costs of immigration exceed its real or potential benefits.[34]

The second approach focuses on racial animosity and posits that opposition is based in prejudice tied to negative feelings about particular ethnic groups, such as Hispanics.[35] Because Hispanics make up the single largest new immigrant group, and because media coverage is twice as likely to specify the ethnicity of Hispanic immigrants as the ethnicity or race of any other group of immigrants, this approach argues that people's views about immigration are tied to their attitudes toward racial minorities and that those who dislike or are prejudiced against Hispanics are more likely to oppose immigration in general.

Research by Brader, Valentino, and Suhay finds more support for the racial animosity interpretation than for the economic self-interest one. They undertook experiments in which participants were exposed to information about the costs and benefits of immigrants who come either from Latin America or Europe. They found that that news coverage emphasizing the costs of immigration increased white opposition more when the immigrants were identified as Latino than when they were identified as European. The authors concluded that group cues can trigger anxiety "independently of the actual threat posed by the group."[36]

The researchers also noted the interplay of news coverage and public opinion. Stories that focused on the costs of immigration *and* that identified the immigrants as Latino produced the greatest opposition to immigration among readers. Those who were worried about costs and focused on Latino immigrants are the ones most anxious about immigration and most likely to see the problem as severe. These types of attitudes also led them to be willing to support English-only policies as a way to respond to the flood of new immigrants. These findings mean that news coverage of the type documented in the last chapter has a discernible impact on public opinion, both on immigration and in other policy areas.[37]

THE LEVEL OF IMMIGRATION

How many immigrants should be allowed into the country is a crucial aspect of public policy.[38] Americans long have held volatile attitudes regarding the overall number of immigrants that should be permitted. Periods of divisive public debates over immigration and problem cases that generate extensive press coverage are associated with calls for restricting the number of immigrants; at other times, the country has been willing to increase the number of immigrants it welcomes.[39]

Table 5-1 shows that in 1953, when the Roper Poll first asked whether immigration should be increased or decreased, 39 percent felt it should be decreased, 13 percent believed it should be increased, and 37 percent wanted to keep it at the same level.[40] This represented a period when public opinion was most favorable to immigration. The United States had won World War II, and the subsequent economic boom and evidence that German

TABLE 5-1. Public Opinion on Desired Immigration Levels

Percent who preferred that immigration level

Year	Remain same level	Increased	Decreased
1953	37	13	39
1965	39	7	33
1977	37	7	42
1986	35	7	49
1993	27	6	65
1995	24	7	65
1999	41	10	44
2000	41	13	38
2001	41	10	43
2001	30	8	58
2002	36	12	49
2003	37	13	47
2004	33	14	49
2005	34	16	46
2006	35	15	47
2007	35	16	45
2008	39	18	39
2009	32	14	50

Source: 1953 Roper Center poll and 1965–2009 Gallup polls.

and other foreign-born scientists had contributed to the American success put the country in a mood that recognized the value of immigration. These individuals had helped America harness the power of the atom and find other scientific breakthroughs that made the country a world leader in science and technology.

In subsequent Gallup Poll surveys, however, the share of people saying they wanted less immigration started to rise and reached a high point of 65 percent in 1993 and 1995, fueled in part by national news stories about Haitians with AIDS who had migrated to the United States and by a wave of violent crime and illegal drugs that plagued Miami and other ports of entry.[41]

By 2007 antagonism to immigration seemed to be abating; the share of those who wanted lower immigration levels had fallen to 45 percent, twenty percentage points lower than the figures from a decade earlier. A year later, the share of Americans wanting less immigration fell to its lowest point in more than fifty years. Just two of every five Americans said they favored lower immigration levels—the same share as in 1953. Many Americans had apparently been reassured that national leaders had heard their concerns about border security and were pouring billions into physical fences, electronic monitors, and increased patrols along the Mexican boundary.

However, the 2008–09 recession drove support for immigration down. Amid the dismal economic news and double-digit unemployment levels, 50 percent of Americans felt immigration should be decreased, 32 percent believed it should be kept at its current level, and 14 percent thought it should be increased.[42] As discussed elsewhere, this uptick in public anxiety is typical in a recession. When people are worried about jobs and economic security, they become more fearful and angry and therefore less likely to support immigration.[43]

According to the 2009 Gallup Poll, Republicans were the most likely to feel that immigration should be decreased. Sixty-one percent of GOP identifiers felt that way, compared with 44 percent of Democrats and 46 percent of independents. This finding suggests clear partisan differences in views about immigration policy and helps explain why legislators rarely reach consensus on this topic.[44]

IS IMMIGRATION GOOD OR BAD FOR THE COUNTRY?

Other surveys have examined whether Americans feel immigration is a good or bad thing for the country as a whole. For example, an analysis of Gallup national public opinion surveys undertaken by writer E. J. Dionne Jr. found that between 2001 and 2007, a majority of Americans believed immigration was a good thing for the country.[45] The number dropped a bit immediately following 9/11 and in 2007 during the national debate over immigration reform. People were a little more reluctant at those times to favor immigration because of increased security concerns. But even in 2007, during a major national debate over comprehensive reform featuring combative rhetoric and conflicting policy views, 60 percent of Americans still felt that new arrivals offered benefits to the country. They recognized that immigrants contributed to the social, cultural, and intellectual vitality of the United States and that they added crucial doses of innovation and entrepreneurship to the American workforce.

There were interesting differences, however, by ethnic group. Seventy-four percent of Hispanics thought immigration was a good thing, compared with 59 percent of non-Hispanic whites and 55 percent of African Americans. The nineteen percentage point difference between African Americans and Hispanics reflects the former's fears that new arrivals take jobs from them and the latter's understanding of the positive contributions of immigrants to American life.

Minority residents clearly draw significant distinctions depending on their personal experiences. The fact that African Americans are least likely to feel positively about immigration demonstrates the importance of economic and social circumstances in people's views. African Americans routinely experience racial prejudice and job discrimination and therefore worry about job competition and economic well-being. These fears undermine their support of immigration and complicate efforts at immigration reform.

In 2009, in the midst of deep recession, the percentage of people believing immigration was a good thing for the United States dropped from 64 to 58 percent. At the same time, the number thinking it was a bad thing rose from 30 percent in 2008 to 36 percent. These trends clearly suggest the challenges facing policymakers when economic conditions are weak.

VARYING VIEWS BASED ON COUNTRY OF ORIGIN

People's feelings about immigration vary considerably depending on the immigrants' country of origin. A 2006 Gallup national survey found the strongest opposition was voiced to migration from Latin America. Forty-eight percent of Americans felt that too many immigrants were coming from Latin American nations, compared with 39 percent who felt that way about Arabic nations, 31 percent who said there were too many Asian immigrants, and 20 percent who believed too many were arriving from Europe.

The clear differential between European and Latin American locales shows clearly that Americans do not feel the same about all immigrants. They are much less concerned about new arrivals who look and act more like themselves than they are about immigrants with different racial, ethnic, and cultural backgrounds. Some of these differences may be attributable to concerns that many Latino migrants are here illegally.

LOW RANKING OF IMMIGRATION AS
THE COUNTRY'S MOST IMPORTANT PROBLEM

Immigration is highly controversial among the general public.[46] As shown in earlier sections, people feel a range of differing sentiments on that subject, and their views vary with the country of origin of the new arrivals, immigration restrictions being contemplated, experiences taking place in their personal lives, and news being reported on immigration and immigrants. Based on this profile, one might expect immigration to be an intense subject for the typical resident.[47]

But immigration does not rank highly in the public mind on America's list of most important problems. In 2008, for example, only 4 percent of Americans on an open-ended question claimed immigration was the country's most important problem. At that time, Congress had addressed many of the border security concerns that had troubled the public, comprehensive reform legislation was off the table, and the economy still was perceived as relatively strong.

Indeed, the only time since 1997 that the public has elevated its ranking of the importance of the issue was in 2006 during the congressional debate over immigration. At that time, 19 percent cited it as the most important problem. Criticisms from both the left and the right led more Americans to feel there were serious problems in this area. The right was worried about border enforcement, while the left felt the federal government was enforcing immigration laws unfairly and selectively.

Since 2006 the share of citizens citing immigration as the most important problem has dropped back to single digits. Overall, the public is much more focused on jobs, the economy, and health care than on immigration reform. The relatively small percentage who place immigration reform at the top of the nation's agenda tend to be concentrated in border states that bear the brunt of illegal immigration.

Unlike some responses on immigration issues that vary with the way the question is asked, the low ranking of immigration reform as the top national priority does not depend on how the question is worded. For example, the Pew Center asked the same question as Gallup about national priorities. But rather than requiring people to volunteer responses, it gave a list of twenty different issues and asked individuals to determine whether each one was a top national priority. In 2009 respondents to the Pew survey put immigration near the bottom of the list of the country's problems. Whereas 85 percent thought the economy should be the top priority, 82 percent named jobs, 76 percent cited terrorism, and 63 percent identified Social Security, only 41 percent stated that immigration should be our country's most important policy priority.[48] Indeed, of the twenty issues, dealing with illegal immigration was ranked seventeenth, above concerns about lobbyists, trade policy, and global warming.

Economic and security issues rank as top priorities because they affect the well-being of virtually everyone. In contrast, immigration generates strong feelings among some individuals, especially those in border states. But for many Americans immigration issues are of secondary importance and immigration policy is not seen as having many significant ramifications for their economic, social, or personal condition.

IMPORTANCE TO ELECTORAL VOTING

Americans may not perceive immigration as one of the country's most important issues, but immigration does rank high on the list of issues that influence voting behavior. There is evidence that voters are willing to cast ballots based on this issue and that people attach considerable importance to this subject at election time. That gives immigration issues great saliency for politicians seeking election or reelection.

During the 2008 election, for example, a *Washington Post/ABC News* survey asked how important a variety of issues were to an individual's vote. Sixty-three percent said that immigration was important to their ballot decision. Issues ranking higher were the economy (92 percent), the Iraq war (83 percent), education (81 percent), health care (78 percent), and taxes (70 percent). Issues ranked less important than immigration included global warming (58 percent), gun control (50 percent), and social issues such as abortion and gay civil unions (39 percent).

Based on his analysis of opinion data, Dionne concluded that "Americans are philosophically pro-immigrant but operationally in favor of a variety of restrictions." The relatively high importance that immigration holds for voters means politicians must pay close attention to their constituents on this issue. Regardless of where immigration is on the national policy agenda, when people say the matter has a high likelihood of affecting their vote, most candidates are going to be very careful not to stray too far from constituent sentiments on this issue.

DIFFERING OPINIONS ON IMMIGRATION RESTRICTIONS

Overall, a majority of Americans worry that illegal immigrants gain access to public services for which they do not pay. When asked in 2008 whether illegal immigrants pay their fair share of taxes or cost taxpayers too much money, 63 percent said they cost too much and only 31 percent said they believed illegals covered their fair share of taxes. At the same time, though, the vast majority of citizens—79 percent—also think that illegal newcomers take low-paying positions that Americans do not want.[49]

Americans draw interesting and sometimes contradictory distinctions regarding potentially tighter immigration policies. For example, a Democracy Corp. study found in December 2007 that 80 percent of a national sample expressed support for tough enforcement of employment sanctions to keep businesses from hiring illegal workers. At the same time, 77 percent said the number of border patrol agents along the Mexico boundary should be doubled, 76 percent favored a guest worker program that would grant temporary visas to immigrants to work in the United States for a set period of time, 65 percent said illegal immigrants should be ineligible for nonessential public services such as welfare programs, 64 percent said illegal immigrants should become eligible to apply for citizenship after they had paid a fee and learned English, 52 percent said all illegal immigrants should be deported, and 51 percent supported the building of a fence along the U.S.-Mexico border.[50]

Similar distinctions emerge when people are asked whether illegal immigrants should be eligible to receive particular public services. For example, 74 percent of Americans believe that children of illegal immigrants should have access to public schools from kindergarten through secondary school. The high percentage of support in this area clearly reflects the strong sentiment among the American public about the importance of education to individual fulfillment and long-term economic well-being. The centrality of education to the American Dream is so strong and pervasive that three-quarters of individuals in the United States are willing to extend this basic right to children of illegal immigrants.

Americans are not as generous, however, when it comes to other policy areas or older children and adults. Only 64 percent favor allowing children of illegals to use hospitals and emergency rooms. And while there is widespread support for early education for children who are in the country illegally, only 50 percent support public education at the high school level for such children. Popular support drops precipitously when it comes to access to higher education, driver's licenses, and government health programs. For example, only 35 percent approve of entrance to state colleges at in-state tuition rates for children of illegal immigrants even if these children are citizens; only 31 percent support driver's licenses for illegal immigrants; and only 25 percent favor access to Medicaid, the government health program for poor people. These contrasts demonstrate that Americans are able to draw distinctions and reach judgments about areas where they feel children of illegals warrant help versus other areas where they do not. People are more willing to support emergency health care than education or poverty programs for illegal immigrants.

VIEWS ABOUT A PATH TO CITIZENSHIP

A majority of Americans do support creating a "path to citizenship" for illegal immigrants currently in the United States, subject to certain conditions. The most recent figures from a 2009 Pew Research Center survey show that nearly two-thirds (63 percent) of Americans favor such a path for immigrants who pass a background check, pay a fine, and have a job.

There are interesting age differences in this preference, though. Support for legalization is strongest among young people aged 18 to 29 years old (71 percent) and declines with older residents. Sixty-seven percent of those aged 30 to 49 favor legalization, compared with 62 percent of those aged 50 to 64 and 48 percent of those over 65.[51]

Gallup probed this topic more deeply by asking what people thought should be required for illegal immigrants to remain in the United States legally and permanently. Seventy-four percent said undocumented aliens must have lived in the country for at least five years, 57 percent felt they should pay a fine for coming to America illegally, and 89 percent believed they should be required to learn English.[52] When these kinds of conditions are attached to the overall citizenship question, support for citizenship for illegal immigrants is relatively strong.

CITIZEN MISTRUST OF GOVERNMENT

Despite some progress in popular support for immigration, advocates of comprehensive reform should remain cautious because past trends demonstrate that public opposition can rise quickly if high-profile immigration cases raise real or imagined economic or security threats to the United States. Just witness the increased opposition that developed during the recent recession. There is nothing permanent about liberalization among the general public because sentiments can shift dramatically based on political or economic events. This analysis of public opinion shows that it is easy for opponents of immigration to create unfavorable media narratives about immigration and that unsympathetic coverage can sway people's views and affect policymaking.[53]

The most cautionary characteristic of contemporary public opinion surrounding immigration is the high level of citizen mistrust toward government in Washington.[54] Many Americans are deeply cynical about the federal government's motives, effectiveness, and efficiency. Indeed, one of the most fundamental changes in the American public's mood since the 1950s has been the rise of pervasive mistrust. In the mid-1900s, two-thirds of Americans trusted the federal government to do what is right. Today, more than two-thirds mistrust the government in Washington.

This deep and abiding mistrust has profound consequences for immigration. Even if national authorities enact comprehensive reform with tough enforcement and border security, ordinary citizens may not be convinced that the government will follow through with effective action. Cynical people believe that illegal immigrants can easily evade border agents and that government actions will be ineffective at safeguarding public security. In this situation, immigration opponents can easily play to citizen skepticism and undermine popular support for policy reform proposals.

Skeptical people are unlikely to believe the promises of leaders about future actions. Any effort to change state or national immigration laws must deal with this reality. Reform activities must take cognizance of people's worries about government capacity and the effectiveness of public sector follow-through. Unless citizen concerns are addressed, making meaningful changes in national immigration policy will be difficult. For this reason, it is clear that no government action will be successful unless it explicitly addresses the public's mistrust of government.

CHAPTER SIX

POROUS BORDERS AND UNEQUAL JUSTICE

IMPLEMENTATION IS A VITAL PART of any public policy. Regardless of how legislators make decisions, issues always arise over policy administration and the substantive impact of policy in specific areas.[1] Appointed officials have discretion to flesh out the broad principles adopted by Congress with specific regulations and instructions for implementing them. These "street-level bureaucrats" typically have considerable authority to determine how to apply various laws to individual cases.[2] Within the limits set by the legislation, they typically can redirect money, reorient programs, grant exceptions, or apply federal principles in novel sorts of ways.

Jeffrey Pressman and Aaron Wildavsky make these points persuasively in their pathbreaking book, *Implementation.*[3] Taking a series of urban case studies, they demonstrate the gap between the abstract principles enacted by legislators in Washington, D.C., and local implementation of those principles in Oakland, California. When money from President Lyndon Johnson's Great Society program came to Oakland in 1966, agency officials were able to shift policy in various ways based on their creative interpretations of congressional intent. They took money intended for one area and applied it elsewhere.

Bureaucratic redirection is not an isolated behavior. In many government programs, legal discretion allows agency leaders to take advantage of budget "fungibility" and policy flexibility.[4] Fungibility refers to the ability to substitute money from one purpose for another. If the federal government gives a city $5 million for a program that the city is already spending $5 million on, the city may be able to redirect the money devoted to the original program to other uses. Policy flexibility allows leaders to make decisions in individual cases that may extend, reframe, or even contradict the broader legislation.[5] In the case of Oakland, so profound were some of the substantive changes that Pressman and Wildavsky described city implementation as a process of "evolution."

The level of administration is especially important in implementation of immigration policy. Responsibility for immigration is spread across a number of different agencies and levels of government. Federal, state, and local officials are involved in decisionmaking, law enforcement, provision of social services, the judicial system, and administration of the nation's immigration law. These officials frequently have very different conceptions of the "problem" and the "solution," a situation that often leads to lack of coordination and integration of government policies and programs.

Given the decentralization and fragmented nature of policy-making, it is no big surprise that implementation of recent immigration policies has led to charges of unequal justice, selective law enforcement, and an inability to safeguard America's national borders.[6] More so than most policy areas, immigration suffers from lack of coordination, uneven implementation, and inequity in the way different people are treated.

Over the years, often in response to citizen complaints, the United States has constructed a huge bureaucracy to handle various aspects of immigration.[7] The bulk of federal immigration funding goes for border security and enforcement. More than half of immigrants coming to America each year arrive illegally, mostly from Mexico or other Latin American nations. The U.S. Customs and Border Protection, located within the Department of Homeland Security, is the agency that guards the borders against illegal crossings and arrests illegal immigrants who manage to get into the country. It employs over 51,000 agents at various points of entry along the American border. Its fiscal 2008 budget totaled $10.9 billion, with $9.5 billion being appropriated and $1.4 billion collected through user fees.[8]

The U.S. Citizenship and Immigration Services has an annual budget of $2.6 billion, of which $2.5 billion is collected through service fees. It employs 18,000 permanent and contract employees around the globe whose mission is to grant visas and citizenship in a manner that "preserve[s] America's legacy as a nation of immigrants while ensuring that no one is admitted who is a threat to public safety."[9] Its agents have considerable leeway in applying complex legal rules to individual cases.

Judicial services and adjudication, primarily in cases where the government is seeking deportation, account for only a small portion of the overall federal immigration budget. Under the aegis of the Justice Department, some 230 immigration judges spread over fifty courts across the nation handle around 292,000 cases a year. In recent years around 350,000 illegal immigrants have been expelled annually from the United States.[10] The annual budget for the Justice Department's Executive Office for Immigration Review is less than $300 million, a mere fraction of the money spent on border security and enforcement.[11]

In this chapter I review issues related to the administration of American immigration policy. Aside from questions about overall policy itself, a number of practical problems relate to border security, legal justice, and enforcement practices. These issues include how best to reduce the flow of illegal immigrants, how to ensure that those facing deportation proceedings receive fair hearings, and how to ensure fair enforcement of laws requiring employers to verify that their employees are legally in the country. These implementation issues have dramatic consequences for street-level bureaucrats as well as for how immigrants and the general public view overall immigration policy.

Currently, virtually every level of the immigration apparatus is facing serious administrative problems. Virtually no one is happy with the way the system is performing.[12] Some critics believe border security does not receive enough attention or that the money is being spent ineffectively. Others think there are serious inequities in law enforcement, in the way both employment verification and deportation proceedings are handled. Still others say that not enough resources are devoted to helping immigrants learn English and assimilate into the American culture.

While many politicians may sincerely believe that immigration should be restricted and all illegals deported, in a highly politicized environment, some elected officials also have incentives to stoke fear and delay action. They suggest remedies that offer little hope of making a positive difference. Until the administrative challenges are addressed, immigration policy will continue to be a divisive and emotional topic for many people. With implementation under suspicion on virtually every political front, it has been impossible to move immigration policy toward a more reasonable level of discourse. Improving administration of immigration policy is mandatory if political leaders are ever to be able to calm the vitriolic rhetoric and build support for future policy reforms.

SECURING THE BORDERS

The United States has 5,525 miles of border with Canada and 1,969 miles bordering Mexico. This total of 7,494 miles of foreign borders creates enormous challenges for national security. From a practical standpoint, there is no way to prevent someone who really wants to enter the United States illegally from doing so. With thousands of miles of open borders in virtually unpopulated areas, border security is a nearly impossible proposition.

The realistic goal of national policy is to keep illegal population flows as low as possible and to make sure that known criminals or suspected terrorists do not enter the country. Few things aggravate American citizens more than the idea of foreigners slipping over the border without proper authorization and competing for jobs, using government resources, and putting residents at security risk.

Of course, the reality is that a large number of people are living in the United States without proper entry visas. Based on personal intercepts and border surveillance, the U.S. Border Patrol keeps detailed statistics on the number of illegal immigrants entering America each year. According to its figures, 11.9 million individuals are in the United States illegally, most of them from Mexico.[13] These people cross by foot, ford rivers, or enter through organized vehicular caravans run by professional smugglers.

The number of illegal arrivals has dropped significantly over the past thirty years. Whereas the annual number of illegal immigrants arrested was 1.7 million in the mid-1980s, that figure dropped to 1 million in the late 1980s, rose to 1.6 million in 2000, and then dropped to 705,000 in 2008. That was the lowest number of border-crossing arrests since 675,000 were stopped in 1976.[14]

Mexican government information shows the same downward trend in out-migration. The government's 2008 figures indicate a 25 percent decline in total emigration to other countries, primarily the United States. According to its numbers, 226,000 fewer Mexicans left the country in 2008 than in 2007. Policy analysts cite America's weak economy as the primary reason for the drop. According to researcher Jeffrey Passel of the Pew Hispanic Center, "If jobs are not available, people don't come."[15]

Illegal immigration may also have slowed because of the beefed-up border security.[16] In recent years the number of border patrol agents stationed along the border with Mexico has been increased by more than 50 percent, from 11,032 in 2006 to 17,415 in 2009 (table 6-1). This increase is remarkable because it took place

TABLE 6-1. Border Patrol Officers along Southern Border, 1992–2009

Year	Number of officers	Year	Number of officers
1992	3,555	2001	9,147
1993	3,444	2002	9,239
1994	3,747	2003	9,840
1995	4,388	2004	9,506
1996	5,333	2005	9,891
1997	6,315	2006	11,032
1998	7,357	2007	13,297
1999	7,706	2008	15,442
2000	8,580	2009	17,415

Source: Marshall Fitz and Angela Kelley, "Principles for Immigration Reform," Center for American Progress, December 2009.

during a period of fiscal austerity in the U.S. government when budget increases were flat for many domestic agencies.[17]

The government also increased the physical barriers aimed at blocking illegal immigrants from crossing the Mexican border. So far 526 miles of fence have been erected in response to legislation passed in 2006 for a 700-mile-long barrier. But building physical barriers represents an expensive solution to the problem of illegal crossings. Government officials in 2007 estimated that construction of 700 miles of a double set of steel fences along the border would cost at least $49 billion and possibly more.[18] Among other items, the estimate included expenditures for labor, construction materials, and purchase of privately owned land, which in some cases might have to be cleared of existing buildings and settlements. Even with that amount of money, the fence would have a life span of only twenty-five years.

The effectiveness of the fencing has also been questioned. A Congressional Research Service report says illegal traffic merely has shifted away from populated areas, where the fences have been built, into unpopulated terrain in the Arizona desert.[19] The result has been an increase in the number of illegals who have died of thirst or exhaustion during their journey to America.

A more cost-effective mechanism would be greater use of cameras and new digital technologies designed to monitor and track unauthorized border crossings. Cameras and remote sensors allow border agents to watch many more miles of border than anyone could do based on physical observation alone. These so-called "virtual fences" have been employed to track undocumented aliens in the busiest corridors, such as south of Tucson, Arizona. Eventually, electronic tools will be deployed along the entire border with Mexico as part of the Secure Borders Initiative. Costing just $6.7 billion, this network of cameras and sensors is far less expensive to develop and operate than other options for safeguarding the border.[20]

In 2010, though, the Obama administration halted work on this virtual fence amidst complaints about "technical problems" and contactor delays. Federal officials cut the fence's budget by 30 percent and shifted money to mobile surveillance devices.[21]

Despite the border security enhancements, legitimate concerns remain among the public at large.[22] President Barack Obama recognized those concerns in early 2009 when he said that it was vital that the United States protect its borders. "If the American people don't feel like you can secure the borders, then it's hard to strike a deal that would get people out of the shadows and on a pathway to citizenship who are already here," he pointed out.[23]

Texas governor Rick Perry pushed the idea of border security one step further. After Web cameras were mounted along part of the Texas border with Mexico, he announced plans to create a "virtual posse" of ordinary citizens who would monitor the cameras and report suspicious activity to authorities. His hope was to harness the collective energy of the public behind law enforcement. In practice, however, his plan has not been very successful. Virtual posses have been hindered by logistical problems of bad camera angles, perspectives that were too distant, and cameras whose images were obscured by bushes or trees. [24] These obstacles have prevented ordinary Americans from helping the U.S. Border Patrol safeguard the security of America's southern boundary with Mexico.

On a larger scale, a group calling itself the Border Fence Project is seeking to build a team of "Cyber Minuteman" enforcers. The nonprofit organization called NoInvaders.org consists of 200,000 members from across the country, who, according to the group's website, view down-streaming video of the southern border; await audible and visual alarms when motion sensors are tripped; and report illegal crossings and activity to the Border Patrol, the police, and nearby Minuteman Ranchers. The latter are local activists who informally police border areas. To sign up through the website, people have to fill out an online questionnaire and provide "correct" answers on at least fourteen of twenty questions advocating tough border enforcement.

Both of these initiatives have been widely criticized by those who fear that virtual posses and cyber minutemen will lead to racial profiling, fraudulent reports, and vigilante justice directed unfairly at certain groups.[25] Civil libertarians support enforcement but want it to be nonselective and based on fair and impartial administrative processes. Having ordinary Americans take the law into their own hands generally has been a recipe for unjust actions. At various points in time, vigilante law enforcement has led to racist actions and brutal outcomes.[26]

Groups monitoring hate crimes, for example, have noted an increase in recent years in incidents targeted on Hispanics. According to the Leadership Conference on Civil Rights Education Fund, hate crimes aimed at Hispanics rose by 40 percent, from 426 incidents in 2003 to 595 incidents in 2007. The group noted that "inflammatory rhetoric" targeted immigrants "at the same time that the number of hate crimes steadily increased against Hispanics and others perceived to be immigrants, heightening a sense of fear in Hispanic and other minority communities around the country.[27]

This increase in incidents directed against Hispanics is noteworthy because the number of overall hate crimes in 2007 actually dropped. In general, crimes based on "dehumanizing, racist stereotypes and bigotry" went down, but those centering on Hispanics represented one of only two categories showing increases (the other being those targeted on gay people).[28] This unfortunate increase demonstrates how calls for virtual posses and vigilante justice can lead to inequitable treatment of Hispanics.

JUSTICE FOR ALL

The judicial system for dealing with illegal immigrants or immigrants who have otherwise violated the terms of their visas is also problematic. The U.S. Department of Justice has set up fifty immigration courts in various locations around the country to handles cases involving illegal entry, migrants who have overstayed their visas, or immigrants who made fraudulent claims when they applied for a visa. Immigration judges appointed by the Justice Department review the evidence and either grant asylum, which allows the person to remain in the United States, or order deportation.[29]

Immigrants are not entitled to counsel to advise them of their rights and to explain the court procedures. Defendants who want a lawyer must pays the costs. Because the hearings are considered civil, defendants have no Fifth Amendment protection against self-incrimination and few of the procedural safeguards associated with American criminal justice. Moreover, many of the defendants face serious language barriers and do not understand the process unfolding before them.[30]

Indeed, studies have found that defendants in 78 percent of the cases do not understand English. With immigrants speaking 389 different languages, requests for translation services are not always fulfilled in a satisfactory manner.[31] When immigrants do not speak English, have no counsel, and do not understand the judicial rules, the end result is quite predictable. Eighty percent of defendants lose their asylum cases and are deported summarily.

A report issued by Fordham Law School found that "demand [for attorneys] outstripped capacity at all levels." This included "initial counseling of immigrants, the delivery of applications for immigrant benefits, the filing of appeals and responding to notices of removal or deportation." The group studying this problem concluded that the immigration system had reached a point of "near-crisis proportions."[32]

Immigration judges are seriously overloaded with cases. The number of proceedings increased from 282,348 in 1998 to an estimated 384,109 in 2009. At the same time, the average amount of time spent on each case dropped from 86 minutes in 1998 and 102 minutes in 1999 to 72 minutes in 2009.[33]

Several problems complicate the administration of justice. First, a 2010 report noted that in March there were forty-eight judgeship vacancies, which is 16 percent of all the judges.[34] Second, in 2008 the typical immigration judge handled 964 cases, or about 20 a week. Moreover, immigration judges receive little help from law clerks or other staff. Whereas federal district judges have two clerks apiece plus a court reporter who keeps a verbatim record of the hearings, immigration authorities have one clerk for every four judges. With little staff help and a heavy case load, the hearings tend to be rushed, with judges having little opportunity to review evidence, call witnesses, listen to transcripts, or request additional information. Judges basically examine the written record and make decisions based on the information placed before them.[35]

An analysis of federal prosecutions shows how quickly immigration cases are handled, compared with other subjects. For example, the typical enforcement involving white-collar crime requires 460 days on average. Narcotics prosecutions generally take 333 days. In contrast to these lengthy proceedings, the average immigration prosecution lasts 2 days. Nearly all immigration cases referred to prosecutors are brought to court, compared with only half of white-collar cases. Many of the latter are settled or dropped.[36]

Large numbers of immigration judges report feeling "frustrated and demoralized" with their jobs. Researchers persuaded ninety-six immigration judges to take a test measuring psychological stress, and most of them scored at the high end of the scale. The researchers found that these judges had stress levels similar to those of prison wardens, another group known to lead high-stress lives. Comments left on the evaluation instrument documented problems such as "an overwhelming volume of cases with insufficient time for careful review, a shortage of law clerks and language interpreters, and failing computers and equipment for recording hearings."[37]

This legal process puts great power in the hands of prosecutors who bring the charges on behalf of the federal government. They compile the evidence from local, state, or federal law enforcement agencies and develop files to be presented to the immigration judges. If the defendant has no legal counsel, the prosecutor's material is the only information available to the judges. A review of immigration court decisions across jurisdictions has found major inequities in the administration of justice. According to one analysis of a Los Angeles immigration court, asylum was approved in almost one-third of the cases (32 percent), but variances across individual judges were large.[38] One judge granted asylum 81 percent of the time, while another granted it only in 9 percent of the cases. Another study found large variations in judicial outcomes for the country as a whole based on the availability of defendant counsel. Those immigrants who had an attorney won their cases 46 percent of the time, compared with a 16 percent success rate for those without a lawyer.[39]

The obvious problem with this variation in the administration of justice is the apparent inequity involved. While objective differences in cases across judges and jurisdictions may account for varying outcomes, the magnitude of the differentials found in these studies raises the possibility that judges are employing different criteria or standards of evaluation. This possibility creates either the perception or the reality of unfairness on the part of those involved with the proceedings. It makes immigrants very cynical about American justice.

Court decisions can be appealed to the Justice Department's Board of Immigration Appeals, a fifteen-judge appellate court. In practice, however, 91 percent of the cases are not appealed.[40] In the small number of cases that are appealed, the appellate court generally does not hold individual hearings or listen to oral arguments. Instead, cases are resolved through a "paper review" of documents associated with the case. Board decisions can be appealed to the U.S. attorney general or to a federal court as a last recourse.

But very few cases go that far. In effect, immigration judges have final authority over whether specific individuals are allowed to stay in the United States or are sent back to their home countries. Such decisions can separate families depending on which members are legal and which are not. The enormity of this choice and the practical impact on families makes for stressful judicial deliberations by these judges.

Since 1999, nearly 2.2 million immigrants have been deported. Of these, 108,434 had children who were lawful American citizens because they were born in the United States. The Department of Homeland Security does not keep data on whether the deportees took their American children with them or left them to live legally in the United States.[41] Under current federal law, immigration judges are not allowed to take family considerations, including the existence of underage children who may be U.S. citizens, into account when making removal decisions.

Surprisingly, there is little media coverage or public awareness of these problems surrounding immigration courts, administrative procedures, and legal justice. Past news reporting has featured a narrative of illegality, in which discussions have centered on illegal immigrants and their costs to society. Yet, one could write a compelling narrative of unfairness in how the United States handles legal proceedings involving immigrants. There are clear inequities based on language status. If you do not understand English, you will not understand the nature of the case against you or be in a position to prepare an adequate defense. In addition, research clearly demonstrates that having a lawyer during removal proceedings dramatically increases your odds of case success. And there is selective enforcement of the law that is problematic. Some individuals, businesses, and communities are singled out for harsh treatment, compared with others that are ignored or receive softer law enforcement.

The integration of immigrants into American society depends upon the fair and efficient administration of justice.[42] People need to perceive that they have a fair shake in legal proceedings and that judges and law enforcement agents are acting equitably. When accused immigrants do not receive the same standard of justice as other people, they feel victimized. Such reactions foster resentment that undermines the moral authority of the United States and reduces people's respect for and obedience to American law.[43]

SELECTIVE ENFORCEMENT OF EMPLOYMENT STATUS

One of the most complicated immigration enforcement areas involves the workplace. Illegal immigrants generally come to the United States seeking employment opportunities not available in their home country. Economic disparities between nations drive migration and create incentives to move to other areas, even when the individual does not have lawful permission.

Once illegals make it to the United States, they usually look for work either in the underground economy, where no work authorization is required for employment, or by using fraudulent papers or weak record-keeping on the part of employers to obtain jobs in the formal economy. Industries such as hotels and motels, restaurants, food processing plants, landscaping, and construction are infamous for being likely to hire illegals because they receive little oversight from federal authorities. According to the Pew Hispanic Center, the industries with the highest percentage of unauthorized immigrants are farming (25 percent illegal), building and grounds keeping (19 percent), construction (17 percent), food preparation and serving (12 percent), industrial production (10 percent), and transportation and material moving (7 percent).[44]

Employment at larger businesses typically involves some type of fraudulent identification because these employers are required to confirm citizenship or legal entry through official documents examined before hiring the worker. Fraudulent driver's licenses, Social Security cards, and other kinds of government identification are relatively easy to procure. Indeed, illicit identification papers are something of a growth industry around the United States.

The U.S. Department of Homeland Security has developed a voluntary "e-verify" program for checking employment status. It maintains an electronic database of employment eligibility that allows businesses to validate the authenticity of submitted documents. Employers submit someone's name, address, and identification card number, and the system looks to see if the registration is associated with the proper person. This system potentially offers the means to ensure fair and efficient administration of justice. Because it is linked to databases maintained by other federal agencies, it enables employers to maintain the integrity of their workforce and guarantee that their employees are legal residents of the United States.

Yet only 1 percent of American businesses use this system.[45] Many worry about the accuracy of its databases. Some employers do not want to know the true employment status of their workers because they prefer to use low-paid employees who receive few, if any, health or pension benefits. Others do not want to take the time to go through the process of complying with a federal registry.

The federal government has three options regarding employment checkups. It can ignore unlawful employment, it can target unlawful employees who commit fraud, or it can focus on businesses that knowingly hire illegals. Each of these approaches has obvious trade-offs.

The first option—looking the other way—obviates the need for an expensive enforcement bureaucracy by accepting some level of employment illegality as typical and unavoidable. The downside of this approach, however, is that it creates incentives for breaking the law. In the long run, tolerating illegal immigrants in the workforce simply encourages more illegals to come to the United States to find work.

The second approach emphasizes enforcement by placing the onus on illegal employees who obtain and use false documents to get a job. Perpetrators are identified, prosecuted, and deported from the United States. This option requires an administrative apparatus for identifying suspects and is costly both in time and money. However, its virtue is that it increases incentives to obey the law by penalizing those who work illegally.

The third option focuses on employers. It presumes that businesses are responsible for hiring decisions, so they should be legally and morally culpable when they hire illegals. Penalties range from fines for civil offenses to prison time for repeated criminal offenses. Because there are fewer employers than employees, enforcement costs are lower; it thus makes sense to focus on companies that knowingly hire illegals or that do not put much effort into verifying the status of their workers.

Over the past decade, the federal government overwhelmingly has emphasized the second option. The U.S. Immigration and Customs Enforcement arrest totals rose from 510 in 2002 to 6,287 in 2008.

Reflecting the probusiness orientation of the Republican administration in office at the time, only 135 of the 6,287 people arrested "were 'owners, managers, supervisors, or human resources employees.'"[46] All the rest (98 percent) were workers.

Many of these arrests were the result of surprise raids by customs authorities on companies thought to be employing illegals. Government authorities targeted a few workplaces, swooped in with dozens of law enforcement agents, and prosecuted individuals who lacked proper documentation of their immigration status. Parents with young children were arrested and placed in confinement. These raids attracted considerable media attention, particularly in the community where the affected jobsite was located. Television cameras recorded the arrests, and newspaper stories documented what happened.

But this focus on illegal workers is problematic at several levels. First, many companies that employ illegal aliens are overlooked, while others are raided and prosecuted. It is not clear why some businesses are singled out for unannounced raids. This angers both the business and the immigrant communities and contributes to perceptions of bias and unfairness in the overall enforcement system.

Second, administrative raids place the onus of employment enforcement on employees as opposed to businesses themselves. Even though employers are the ones who hired the workers and certified their employment documents, they face relatively low sanctions or legal penalties. This does little to penalize bad behavior on the part of employers or to create incentives for them to abide by the rules.

Third, the separation of parents from children following these raids creates humanitarian hardships. Illegal workers generally are incarcerated immediately following the raids. According to government statistics for 2002–08, the average incarceration period for arrested workers was thirty-seven days.[47] Mothers and fathers might send their children off to school one morning, be arrested later that day, and not be in a position to take care of the kids for more than a month. This disruption in family lives is a source of great outrage in the immigrant community.

A recent *Washington Post* story documented the arbitrariness of at least some of the government raids. According to the news account, customs enforcement teams were given annual quotas of 1,000 arrests of undocumented immigrants. When one set of agents came back with few arrests from a January 2007 night searching for criminal immigrants, their supervisor ordered the group out to secure more arrests. Pulling into a 7-Eleven store in Baltimore, they noticed a group of Hispanic men and arrested twenty-four individuals. None had given any indication of criminal activity, and many of them had not even talked to the officers before being arrested. The story concluded with the critical line that "the detainees were hardly the threats to the United States that the team was designed to focus on."[48]

Despite all the personal hardships and business disruptions of employment raids, the federal government netted only 1,103 criminals and 5,200 employees working illegally during 2008. Given the high costs of government raids, this "yield" is disappointing. Considerable money and time is required to execute the raids, and these actions create understandable unhappiness and ill will among businesses and the immigrant communities. That few of those arrested were business owners or executives suggests that the federal government has gone lighter on employers than employees. All things considered, the raids have not been particularly effective in enforcing the law against hiring illegal immigrants.

As a result, the Obama administration has shifted focus and now is targeting employers rather than workers, placing the onus on the people who are supposed to guarantee the authenticity of employment authorizations.[49] Befitting its orientation toward labor and working-class individuals, the administration is auditing companies thought to be hiring illegal workers. Rather than focusing on individual offenders, it is going after the businesses that employ them and subjecting their owners and officers to civil prosecution.

An example of this new approach came in 2009 when the newly elected Obama administration sent Los Angeles company American Apparel a letter informing it that 1,800 of its 5,600 employees were illegal immigrants without proper work permits. Rather than coming in with dozens of agents, law enforcement officials warned the company that it would be the subject of civil fines and needed to verify the employment status of its workers. The press account for this story noted that federal agents planned to focus on "businesses employing large numbers of workers suspected of being illegal immigrants."[50] The government, it said, intended to target big businesses and reserve criminal charges for repeat offenders and intentional violations.

That same day, the federal government mailed similar letters to 652 other businesses warning them of possible hiring violations. Each company was given thirty days to respond to the complaint. Employees who were not able to verify their work status during that time period would be terminated. No workers were arrested and no high-profile press conferences called. The government simply treated the matter as a routine regulatory enforcement.

Administration agencies also are checking the identification and fingerprints of criminals in custody to see if any are in the United States unlawfully. A pilot program set up by the Department of Homeland Security found that around 10 percent of the prisoners surveyed were illegal immigrants. With a total national incarceration of 14 million people, the department estimated that there would be 1.4 million "criminal aliens" who could be deported across the country—ten times the 117,000 criminals deported in 2008.[51]

The way the government administers immigration issues matters a great deal to how citizens and immigrants alike see the public sector. The government's ineffectiveness in dealing with enforcement and judicial issues has made it difficult to build confidence both among the immigrant community and the American public at large. Immigrants believe the country is too hard on undocumented workers and too easy on employers who knowingly hire them, while many Americans feel that illegal immigrants should be penalized for breaking the law. Until this status quo is altered, each set of people will feel that the current system is unfairly biased.

CONCLUSION

To summarize, immigration policy is poorly administered in several key respects. People worry about the implementation of border security, legal justice, and enforcement practices, among other things. Reducing the flow of illegal immigrants has been challenging. There are differential outcomes for those facing deportation proceedings depending on whether they have legal representation. Selective enforcement of employment rules has led to resentment among both immigrants and employers.

The sad fact is that practically no one is happy with the administration of the country's immigration laws.[52] This is true across businesses that employ low-skilled labor, high-tech companies, higher education, law enforcement, social service agencies, the immigrant community, and government itself. People experience different realities depending on which part of the overall system they deal with. But many parts of it are especially problematic from the ground level where laws actually are enforced.

These issues are not unique to the immigration area. Implementation and administration problems affect nearly every area of public policy. Large organizations are often inefficient and ineffective. Most agencies encounter difficulties in putting legislative directions into effect. But until the government resolves the challenges of effectively implementing laws pertaining to undocumented people in the United States, native-born Americans and their elected representatives will continue to be divided on immigration issues.

CHAPTER SEVEN

THE EINSTEIN PRINCIPLE

IN THIS BOOK I HAVE argued that Americans and their policymakers need to rethink immigration policy. The centerpiece of the current policy is family reunification. Nearly two-thirds of the 1 million visas granted each year are set aside to reconnect family members.[1] That is a noble and virtuous goal, but such a strong emphasis on one policy objective slights competing principles such as economic development, international competitiveness, and technological innovation. Immigration policy is seriously out of balance and needs fundamental change if it is to achieve important national objectives.

Only in the past forty years has family unification been elevated to its current dominant position. For most of American history, the country alternated between relatively open borders that encouraged immigration (1789 to 1924) and restrictive policies that discouraged immigration (1924 to 1965). This shift reflected changing national priorities as the nation moved from a need for population growth to one where immigration was widely perceived as a threat to economic and physical security.

In neither of those earlier periods, though, was immigration policy as focused on family considerations as it is today. During nearly 150 years of open borders, for example, the nation allowed entry based on any consideration, such as the desire for political freedom, religious expression, land, economic development, or reunification with loved ones. Even when immigration policies became more restrictive during the twentieth century, visas were still granted for the purposes of providing useful employment and needed skills.

On some occasions the United States worried about particular immigration threats so much that it singled out specific groups for harsh treatment, such as the Chinese in the 1800s, the Japanese during World War II, and Arabs following the September 11, 2001, terrorist attacks.[2] This focus unbalanced U.S. immigration policy because leaders elevated national security linked to particular groups as the primary consideration in admissions decisions and downplayed other considerations.

After looking at information on policy principles, institutional processes, public opinion, media coverage, and administrative enforcement, I suggest that American citizens and policymakers need to reconceptualize immigration as a brain gain for the United States. The country needs to reduce illegal immigration and strengthen legal immigration in ways that draw top international talent on the order of Albert Einstein, the immigrant scientist whose advances in nuclear physics contributed so much to the country's national defense.[3]

Care must be taken that any immigration reforms do not produce class, racial, or ethnic biases. The smart kid from a low Indian caste deserves the same consideration as a white engineer from the United Kingdom. National policy should make room for smart, creative, and innovative individuals from Asia, Africa, and Latin America, not just Europe. It should recognize that poor and working-class students often are highly motivated and therefore deserving of consideration for entry into the United States.

There are challenges for particularistic politics, jingoistic media coverage, polarized public opinion, and unfair administration. In many respects, immigration is a social, economic, intellectual, and cultural benefit for the country as a whole.[4] National policy needs to recognize the past contributions that newcomers have made and facilitate the arrival of other immigrants who will bring equally important virtues to the United States.[5]

Given America's long-term national ambivalence toward immigration, political leaders have found it difficult to resolve conflict and make reasonable policy decisions.[6] The last time Congress sought to deal with immigration in 2006 and 2007, the effort ended up in a hopeless political stalemate. Neither the left nor the right was willing to make compromises that were necessary to produce comprehensive changes in national policy.

In this chapter I argue that rather than repeating past arguments about immigration and continuing to ignore important concerns from various parts of the political spectrum, it is time to reconfigure policy in new sorts of ways. Border security must be taken seriously. Employment verification must be tightened through the e-verify program, with an appeals process added for fairness. The judicial system for administering immigration laws must be improved. An independent commission should be established that can depoliticize conflict over immigration policy. Immigration levels should be tied to national economic cycles, and stronger steps should be taken to integrate new immigrants into American life.

Taken together, these ideas offer the potential to create a government policy that serves important national interests and puts America on a stronger course for the future. Immigration policy that better balanced employment needs and family reunification would encourage innovation, make the United States more competitive internationally, and enhance the nation's long-term economic prosperity. And by being clearer about national objectives, policy changes along the lines suggested here would defuse public concerns and increase citizen support for American immigration. These policy changes would rebalance perceptions about costs and benefits and make sense to a majority of Americans both from a policy and a political standpoint.

A NEW NARRATIVE:
RECONCEPTUALIZING IMMIGRATION AS A BRAIN GAIN

The most important challenge is to develop a new narrative that defines immigration as a brain gain that improves economic competitiveness and national innovation. A focus on brains and competitiveness would help America overcome past deficiencies in immigration policy and help the country meet the economic and innovation challenges of the twenty-first century.[7]

There is considerable evidence that the United States is falling behind on innovation.[8] An analysis of patents granted shows that the long-term U.S. dominance has come to an end. In 1999 American scientists were granted 90,000 patents, compared with 70,000 for those from all other countries. In 2009, for the first time in recent years, non-U.S. innovators earned more patents (around 96,000) than did Americans (93,000).[9]

One-third of the American workforce holds science or technology positions. That is slightly less than the 34 percent figure for Germany and the Netherlands but is higher than the 28 percent in Canada and France. Looking at another measure, the U.S. government spends only 2.8 percent of its GDP on public research and development. That is less than the 4.3 percent spent by Sweden, 3.1 percent by Japan, and 3.0 percent by South Korea but is more than is spent by Germany (2.5 percent), France (2.2 percent), Canada (1.9 percent), or England (1.9 percent). Europe as a whole devotes 1.9 percent of its total GDP to research and development, while industrialized nations spend around 2.3 percent.[10]

In the early 1960s the federal government provided more than three-fifths of all research and development spending, while the private sector accounted for about 30 percent and other money came from non-U.S. sources. In 1980 the private sector in the

United States surpassed the federal government in the amount of money spent on research and development. By 2003 private companies were providing 60 percent of the $283 billion spent on research and development, compared with 40 percent from the federal government. Of this total, $113 billion comes from the federal government, while $170 billion comes from the private sector.[11]

Meanwhile the demand for those with science and engineering expertise is increasing, but the United States is falling behind in producing sufficient knowledge workers. Thirty-eight percent of Korean students now earn degrees in science and engineering, compared with 33 percent of German students, 28 percent of French, 27 percent of English, 26 percent of Japanese, and just 16 percent of American graduates.[12]

To boost American innovation, current immigration policy contains a provision for a visa "brains" program. The so-called "genius" visa, formally known as O-1, allows the government to authorize visas for those having "extraordinary abilities in the arts, science, education, business, and sports." In 2008 around 9,000 genius visas were granted, up from 6,500 in 2004. The idea, similar to earlier programs, is to encourage talented people to migrate to America.

However, this program is small, and entry passes have gone to individuals such as professional basketball player Dirk Nowitzki of Germany, various members of the Merce Cunningham and Bill T. Jones/Arnie Zane dance companies, and other prominent people.[13] While these people clearly have special talents, the program should be expanded and also targeted on people who create jobs and further American technological innovation.

The little-known EB-5 visa program is a positive example of a way to tie U.S. immigration policy to job creation. It offers temporary visas to foreigners who invest at least $500,000 in American locales officially designated as "distressed areas." If their financial investment leads to the creation of ten or more jobs, the temporary visa automatically becomes a permanent green card. In 2008, 945 immigrants provided over $400 million through this program—without receiving much media attention.[14] On a per capita basis, these benefits make the program one of the most successful economic development initiatives in the federal government.

Building on the same principle as the EB-5 visa, Senators John Kerry (D-Mass.) and Richard Lugar (R-Ind.) have introduced legislation known as the StartUp Visa Act for foreign entrepreneurs. It would provide a two-year visa for foreigners able to attract at least $250,000 in business capital from American investors. If a foreign entrepreneur created at least five full-time jobs from this money during the two-year visa period, exceeded $1 million in revenues, or raised more than $1 million in new capital, he or she could become a permanent resident.[15]

If a goal of national policy is to encourage investment and job creation, targeted visas of this sort are very effective. They explicitly link new immigration with concrete economic investment. They also generate welcome capital for poor geographic areas. There is public accountability for this policy program because the temporary entry visas become permanent only after a specified number of jobs have been created.

U.S. immigration policy should be imbued with what I think of as the "Einstein Principle." In this perspective national leaders would give greater priority in the visa line to those with brains, talent, and special skills in order to attract more individuals with the potential to enhance American innovation and competitiveness. The goal is to boost the national economy by bringing individuals to America who have the potential to make significant contributions.

Right now, only 15 percent of annual visas (about 150,000) are set aside for employment purposes. Of these, some go to seasonal agricultural workers, while a small number of H-1B visas (65,000) are reserved for "specialty occupations" such as scientists, engineers, and technological experts. Individuals admitted with this work permit can stay for up to six years and are able to apply for a green card if their employer is willing to sponsor their application.

The number reserved for scientists and engineers is drastically below the figure allowed between 1999 and 2004. In that interval, the federal government set aside up to 195,000 visas each year for H-1B entry. The idea was that scientific innovators were so important for long-term economic development that the number set aside for those specialty professions needed to be high. But that number reverted back to 65,000 in 2004.

Today most of the 65,000 visas are allocated within a few months after they become available at the start of the government's fiscal year in October. Even in the recession-plagued period of 2009, visa applications exceeded the supply within the first three months of the fiscal year. American companies were responsible for 49 percent of the H-1B visa requests in 2009, up from 43 percent in 2008. The companies awarded the largest number of these visas included both American firms and foreign firms with American subsidiaries. Among them were Wipro (1,964 visas), Microsoft (1,318), Intel (723), IBM India, Patni Americas (609), Larsen & Toubro Infotech (602), Ernst & Young (481), Infosys Technologies (440), UST Global (344), and Deloitte Consulting (328).[16] Clearly, the demand for high-skilled immigrant workers is higher than the allowed supply. One way to get a start on the brain gain would be to bring the number of visas for high-skilled workers back up to 195,000 a year.

LEARNING FROM OTHER NATIONS
ABOUT THE PURSUIT OF SKILLED WORKERS

Other countries such as Canada, the United Kingdom, and Australia are more strategic in viewing immigration as a way to attract foreign talent. Canada, for example, explicitly targets foreign workers to fill positions for which there are not enough skilled Canadians. Under a point system, prospective immigrants accumulate points toward admission based on field of study, educational attainment, and employment experience. Once a person acquires a certain level of points based on desired employment qualities, he or she is granted a visa.

Canada aims to admit around 265,000 immigrants each year. Of these, 154,000 visas (58 percent) are set aside for economic purposes, such as skilled workers or live-in caregivers; 71,000 (26 percent) are set aside for family reunification. Indeed, the Canadian skilled-worker classification constitutes 36 percent of all immigrant visas, much higher than the 6.5 percent share in the United States.[17]

Canada's percentages are nearly the reverse of national policy in the United States, where visas for family reunification far outweigh those allocated for employment. Unlike other countries whose leaders understand the value of skilled immigrant labor and occupations in short domestic supply for long-term economic development, the United States persists in putting a low priority on admitting immigrants with special talents.

One of the results of the Canadian approach is that immigration is far less controversial among the general public than it is in the United States because Canadian citizens see how newcomers strengthen the national economy. With benefits spelled out clearly, the cost-benefit ratio is perceived as being very favorable for the country as a whole. The Gallup Organization confirmed this perception with polling it conducted in 2005 about public views of immigration in Canada, the United States, and Great Britain. In the United States and Great Britain, where immigration is more family-based, opposition to immigration was intense. Fifty-two percent of Americans and 65 percent of the British said they wanted to decrease immigration. In contrast, in Canada, where national policy focuses on economic goals, only 27 percent of residents wanted to decrease immigration. Most wanted to keep it the same (52 percent), and 20 percent felt that immigration levels should be increased. The latter number is much higher than the 7 percent of Americans and 5 percent of British who wanted to raise immigration in their respective countries.[18]

These cross-country survey results demonstrate the tie between policy goals and public opinion. When countries target clear benefits in their national immigration policy, the general public responds favorably. This policy configuration makes the benefits of immigration easier to see, and citizen concerns regarding possible costs decline accordingly. The United States has put itself in a difficult political position because it has so many illegal immigrants in addition to the large number of legal immigrants it admits each year. Instead of viewing immigration as a brain gain, Americans tend to see the costs as broad and the benefits are narrow.

In this situation, it is not a big surprise that many feel the United States has an unfavorable cost-benefit policy ratio. Public opinion responds to the broad contours of national public policy. If the policy is unclear about the national benefits, people will have difficulty seeing the policy results in a positive light. Their views will take on the qualities seen in American public opinion: skepticism, negativity, and resentment about new arrivals.

Government policy should encourage positive, not negative, public opinion. If citizens are to support immigration, the national benefits of immigration must be obvious to them. The problem with today's policies is that they focus public and media attention much more on the costs than the benefits, which in turn makes the policies controversial and emotional for so many people.

Many congressional leaders do not fully grasp how public policy contributes to unsympathetic public opinion. They focus on immigrant costs and therefore encourage media coverage that frames reporting in a negative direction. That stimulates anxiety, fear, and skepticism from the general public and leads people to become even less favorable toward immigration. For example, proposed legislation by Senators Dick Durbin (D-Ill.) and Charles Grassley (R-Iowa) would move the United States even further away from where it needs to be. Their bill would restrict most companies from using employment-based visas. Companies with more than fifty workers would not be able to recruit additional employees with H-1B visas if more than half of their workforce already is composed of H-1B or L-1 visa holders targeted for workers at international companies with U.S. offices needing to bring foreign workers to America for up to three years. Designed to limit competition with American workers, this bill would place new caps on a program that already is very restrictive.[19]

This legislation represents a step in the wrong direction because it limits high-skill recruitment. Lamenting the shortage of skilled labor, Craig Barrett, then the chairman of Intel, said, "We are watching the decline and fall of the United States as an economic power." American schools are not producing enough graduates with science and technical abilities. Meanwhile, a ready pool of talent is available—graduates who grew up in other countries but were educated in the United States. But instead, they are sent home after graduation with no opportunity for American employment. "With a snap of the fingers, you can say, 'I'm going to make it such that those smart kids—and as many of them as want to—can stay in the United States,'" Barrett noted. "But instead of keeping them in America, we say, 'They're here today, they're graduating today—and they're going home today.'"[20]

AUTOMATIC GREEN CARDS FOR FOREIGN GRADUATES OF AMERICAN SCIENCE AND TECHNOLOGY PROGRAMS

A similar complaint was made by New York City mayor Michael Bloomberg, who recognized the shortsightedness of U.S. policy during an appearance on NBC's *Meet the Press*. "We do the stupidest thing—we give them educations, and then don't give them green cards," Bloomberg said.[21] One solution to this problem would be the creation of a "green card" track for foreign graduates of American science, technology, engineering, and math programs. Such a program would encourage international students graduating from American universities to stay in the United States and help to realize a return on the thousands of dollars spent on their training and on developing their skill levels.

Leading private universities cost more than $50,000 a year. For an undergraduate student, the cost of getting a degree is over $200,000. For those pursuing a Ph.D., the expense can run over $250,000, and much of this cost is covered by universities seeking to attract smart students from abroad. Yet despite these extraordinary investments, little effort is made to keep these knowledge workers in the United States.

The need to retain trained graduates is especially important in the areas of science, technology, engineering, and math, fields in which fewer and fewer American students are pursuing degrees. Research documents that foreign graduates start businesses and become successful entrepreneurs.[22] Many of them would love to stay in the United States if they could do so legally.

For this reason, we need a brains policy explicitly designed to keep top international talent in the United States. Other countries pursue this kind of approach because they understand its importance for long-term competitiveness and economic innovation. Attracting creative and innovative foreigners can be a tremendous boost to the national economy. That kind of policy will stimulate innovation and create new jobs in vital industries.

NARROW THE DEFINITION OF RELATIVES TO IMMEDIATE FAMILY

A challenge of current policy is not just its disproportionate emphasis on family unification but also its expansive definition of relatives that reaches well into the extended family. Immigrants who come to the United States are allowed to sponsor other relatives; once one person arrives in the country, a chain of immigration begins that extends to immediate and then to more distant relatives. As a result, the primary entry requirement of U.S. immigration policy has become blood ties rather than national goals. Between the low number of visas for skilled and seasonal workers and the advantage that family ties have over skill categories, the United States has ended up with a national policy that does not pursue its strategic interests.

For this reason, the Brookings-Duke Immigration Policy Roundtable, composed of academic experts from a wide variety of ideological perspectives, recommended that the definition of family "be narrowed as much as feasible to mean nuclear family members."[23] There are strong social and humanitarian grounds for—and a legitimate national interest in—allowing immigrants to bring their spouses and children together in one household. Abundant sociological evidence shows the benefits of family integration for social and economic outcomes.[24] But little research documents any value in bringing aunts, uncles, cousins, and other distant relatives under the banner of family unification. They also are less vital to the socialization of young children.

Roundtable coordinators estimate that this single policy change would free up at least 160,000 visa slots annually.[25] These visas could be used to admit high-skilled workers, seasonal workers, foreign graduates of American university science and technology programs, or other individuals with special talents that would advance long-term economic development. Such a policy shift would double the number of employment-based visas.

An alternative approach has been put forth in a report issued by the Center for American Progress. The report rejected as a false choice the tension between family versus skill-based admissions. Instead it recommended keeping the current emphasis on family unification and not expanding the visas for employment. But recognizing the long-term economic needs of the nation, it suggested Congress create a new pool of "discretionary" visas to be used to recruit high-skilled workers.[26]

The problem with this approach is that it would boost overall immigration numbers well over the current level of roughly 1 million immigrants a year, an increase that is unlikely to be acceptable to the general public. As noted earlier, recent public opinion surveys have found the percentage of Americans who want to increase immigration to be in the single digits.[27] There simply is no support for an increase in immigration beyond current levels. That leaves national policymakers with the difficult dilemma of figuring out how to limit family-based visas to free up entry visas for economic or employment-related purposes. We need to focus more on employment-based entry programs in order to attract needed talent and create greater political support for immigration as a whole. But reducing the number of family-based visas to increase the number of employment-based visas is exactly the sort of choice that politicians seem unable or unwilling to make.

EARNED LEGALIZATION AS A PATH TO CITIZENSHIP

What to do about the 11.9 million immigrants who are illegally in the United States represents one of the most emotion-laden aspects of the immigration debate. These individuals represent the face of immigration that enrages many native Americans.

It is impractical to engage in mass deportation of these individuals. Undocumented workers account for 5.4 percent of the labor force, or around 8.3 million individuals. Undocumented workers pay $7 billion in Social Security payroll taxes every year.[28] They also produce $144 billion in economic activity.[29] A study by the Center for American Progress estimates that returning illegal immigrants to their home countries would cost nearly $300 billion plus pose massive logistical problems.[30] Deportation on a large scale simply is not viable as a national immigration strategy in the United States.

Public opinion data show that Americans favor a path to citizenship as long as illegal immigrants pay a fine for entering the country illegally, pay any back taxes, pass background checks, and learn English.[31] Most of the American public is opposed to outright forgiveness. Language acquisition is a key ingredient in this "earned legalization" because understanding English helps the individual to get a better job, become integrated into the United States, and appear "less different" from the people already here.[32]

Providing this kind of pathway to citizenship is more acceptable to the American public than "amnesty" because it recognizes the lawbreaking that took place. Providing the right incentives for good behavior is important because it discourages continued lawbreaking or additional people from crossing the border illegally in the future. Requiring illegals to pay a fine and back taxes also helps build popular support because it compensates the United States for past unlawful activity.

If this pathway becomes law, however, the country must be prepared to beef up English instruction and American civics courses. The existing supply of such courses is already inadequate and is not going to accommodate the millions of immigrants who will face a new statutory requirement to learn civics and English. Even if no legislation is enacted, the United States needs to provide more, and more effective, English language instruction. Good quality data and performance measures are critical for understanding whether taxpayer dollars are being used effectively to boost immigrants' social, civic, and economic integration. Press reports indicate that some adult English language providers are losing up to one-third of their budgets because of government funding cutbacks. These spending reductions combined with fiscal pressures at the state and local levels have forced some locales to cut courses or move to lotteries to decide who gets into the remaining classes. The country needs to take English language instruction more seriously if it wants to encourage immigrant integration.

TAKE BORDER SECURITY SERIOUSLY

A key to restoring public confidence in immigration policy is to treat border security seriously. As long as hundreds of thousands of foreigners continue to cross the border unlawfully, Americans are going to have serious problems with immigration policy. Citizens fear that the U.S. government is not effectively patrolling the border and that the country is being overrun by illegal immigrants. These perceptions undermine moral authority and breed disrespect for the law. Unless progress is made on this issue, solving the political controversy surrounding immigration policy will be impossible.

The gravest public concern comes in regard to Mexico. Poverty, violence, and political repression at home bring Mexicans to the United States. The recent wave of drug-related violence that has swept over Mexico and at times spilled into the United States adds considerable urgency to this issue. The United States is unlikely to make much progress on illegal population flows without addressing the special case of Mexico and the issues of drugs and violence.[33] The export of drugs from Latin America into the United States is a serious problem that undermines the country's ability to maintain social order. Mexico and other Latin countries must do a better job of dealing with these issues if public opinion is going to grow more supportive of immigration.

One of the most important challenges in border enforcement is finding techniques that are cost effective. Building physical barriers is enormously expensive. Construction of just 700 miles of fencing—little more than a third of the length of the U.S. border with Mexico—was estimated to cost at least $49 billion, and the estimate did not include maintenance or the costs of replacing the fencing after just twenty-five years. And questions have been raised about the effectiveness of these physical barriers in slowing the flow of illegal immigrants.

In any government program, there must be a reasonable balance between costs and benefits. Citizens must see that large public sector investments are going to yield discernible benefits. A program that is expensive but not very effective breeds further cynicism about government policy. Individuals quickly learn to doubt the government's capacity and long-term ability to solve problems and to question its ability to do any better in the future.

This appears to be the solution that is not working. A better solution is to employ new digital tools such as webcams and remote sensing in a targeted manner to enforce border security. These techniques are far less expensive than fences but still allow law enforcement agents to monitor crossing points and pinpoint areas in need of strict enforcement. The most frequently used crossing points can be targeted for more active enforcement. Remote sensing tools allow government authorities to move these points of emphasis around depending on the greatest need. Border control authorities are starting to do this and getting good results.

TIGHTEN EMPLOYMENT VERIFICATION THROUGH E-VERIFY WITH AN APPEALS PROCESS

People with fraudulent work papers represent a major challenge in the immigration area. Under the current system, where employers must manually check the authenticity of Social Security cards and driver's licenses, detecting skillfully produced faulty papers can be difficult. The typical employer or human resources person has a hard time recognizing good forgeries. As a result, many undocumented newcomers are able to obtain jobs illegally and remain in the United States.

A digital approach that offers some promise on this front is an e-verify system with an appeals process built into it. Under this plan, prospective employers check an electronic database maintained by the U.S. Department of Homeland Security in cooperation with the Social Security Administration. This Internet-based system compares the validity of Social Security numbers with existing databases and certifies whether someone has a legal employment status.

Critics complain that this system tags people as illegal when they actually are not. Current government statistics show that 3.1

percent of employment status inquiries lead to nonconfirmation. Of these, 0.3 percent are found to be inaccurate, while 2.8 percent reflect fraudulent employment claims.[34] For those falsely accused of being illegal, the system can create unnecessary anxiety.

One way to protect against this type of unfairness is to build an appeals process into the system so that anyone identified as being illegal can challenge that decision, present evidence, and get a quick resolution of the disqualification. People singled out for not being validly in the country based on Social Security records should have thirty to sixty days to appeal adverse decisions before losing their job. In this way, the system could balance the need for employment verification with the parallel requirement of fairness and justice in the proceedings. Such an approach would produce a system that is viewed with greater legitimacy by employers and employees alike.

The e-verify system also has been controversial among immigration rights organizations because of questions regarding the accuracy of the databases. It is imperative that government officials clean up databases to ensure accurate processing of employment verification. There is no justification for out-of-date information in government databases. Indeed, government agencies such as Social Security, the Internal Revenue Service, and Workers Compensation boards in individual states have clear incentives to upgrade their record keeping. Beyond the function of employment verification for immigrants, they need excellent records to fulfill their core missions of pension benefits and tax collection.

New technology makes it possible to verify job employment and certify documented workers. As long as government authorities have databases that provide accurate tests of legal status, digital technologies can help defuse one of the most combustible aspects of the current employment process. The move from paper records to electronic databases offers the promise of faster and more accurate processing of employment claims and a way to reassure an American public angry about illegal workers.

IMPROVED LEGAL REPRESENTATION

Adequate attorney representation in immigration courts is desperately needed. Currently, most undocumented defendants lack lawyers, and if they are fortunate to find one, they have to pay for the representation themselves. This creates a two-tiered justice system that is blatantly unfair. Defendants with legal representation have a much higher rate of winning their cases than those who do not. As noted in an earlier chapter, nearly half of those individuals with lawyers win their deportation cases, compared with less than one of every five clients without an attorney.

Language translation in court proceedings is also in short supply. Studies have found that defendants in 78 percent of removal proceedings do not understand English and thus, without a translator, are unable to comprehend what is happening in the courtroom and to prepare a proper defense. This situation calls into question the fairness of deportation proceedings.

The combination of inadequate legal representation and poor language skills means that many deportation cases are one-sided events. Government lawyers present evidence in English, the defendant has no attorney, there are few opportunities to challenge evidence, and the judge makes a quick decision based on the information before him or her. After cases lasting an average of 72 minutes, the judicial result in most proceedings is a speedy deportation for the defendant.

Because the government does not pay for legal representation and because so many defendants cannot afford an attorney, legal professionals are encouraging law firms and nonprofit organizations to provide pro bono representation in immigration cases. This gets around taxpayer objections to spending public money on people thought to have come into the country illegally. Through volunteer attorneys, defendants gain at least some understanding of the evidence against them and of how to prepare a defense. As Robert Katzmann, a federal appellate court judge, explained,

"Justice should not depend on the income level of immigrants."[35] Improving the degree of legal representation and defendant language understanding in immigration cases is mandatory. The one-sided and unfair legal proceedings seen in many cases cannot continue if immigrants are expected to respect the law.

ENHANCE PERFORMANCE TRAINING AND EVALUATION OF IMMIGRATION JUDGES

The judges who decide immigration cases could benefit from better training and evaluation, and more of them. These 230 individuals are chosen by officials in the Department of Justice for two-year terms. They do not have tenure and are not guaranteed reappointment. Good training helps ensure that consistent standards are applied across the country and that judges in various areas do not use different criteria to evaluate cases of similar circumstances.

Recognizing the importance of this point, the Executive Office for Immigration Review has developed several proposals for upgrading training and assessment. In 2008, for the first time, it established performance evaluations that rated immigration and appellate judges; the office also provided training and mentoring on legal and procedural issues.

Annual conferences have been created to disseminate judicial "best practices." And a new *Immigration Judge Benchbook* has been put together to help judicial officials understand how to handle various matters. Procedures to detect poor-quality judges were established, and analysis of disparities in granting asylum was undertaken. Supervisors make field visits to see how various court offices are performing. The office also has announced plans to establish a code of conduct for judges.[36]

Currently, judges have to audiotape proceedings themselves and do not have detailed transcripts, which makes it difficult for them to review evidence and evaluate the material in front of them. Insufficient records of the initial court proceedings and of the basis for the judge's decision are one reason why appeals almost always fail. The Executive Office of Immigration Review has plans to add digital audio recording by the end of 2010, which would allow all courts to have higher-quality recordings of legal proceedings. Digital devices could also help upgrade court records and judicial proceedings, which would help make the appeals process fairer in nature.

Given the number of foreign languages involved in immigration hearings, there is a great need for language interpreters and improved training in this area. The review office has implemented a plan for continuing education and performance reviews for court interpreters, which should help improve defendants' ability to understand the proceedings and defend themselves in immigration cases.

CHECK PRISONER FINGERPRINTS

Another concern of the general public is the potential for serious criminals to cross the border. The problem with such criminals is not only the crimes they perpetrate but the money law enforcement officers spend identifying, capturing, and prosecuting the person in question.

One way to get rid of foreign criminal elements is through systematic prisoner checkups. There are 14 million individuals in prisons and jails across the United States. The Federal Bureau of Investigation estimates that 10 percent of all U.S. prisoners—1.4 million individuals—are "criminal aliens," meaning that they are in America illegally. Under a program that began in the Bush administration, the federal government assesses the immigration status of every prisoner in America. This initiative matches fingerprints to immigration databases to determine whether the culprit should be deported.

In 2008, 117,000 prisoners found to be illegal immigrants were deported from the United States.[37] If FBI calculations are correct, this is only one-tenth the number of criminals who could be removed. However, it is difficult for the government to remove large numbers of people so officials prioritize prisoner removals based on the severity of the crime. Those who are guilty of "level 1" offenses, such as homicide, kidnapping, sexual offenses, robbery, assault, or drug offenses with sentences of a year or more are removed first. According to immigration authorities, local offices have discretion whether to proceed with removal for those guilty of less severe level 2 or 3 offenses. Some prisoners are offered early parole from incarceration in exchange for removal from the United States.[38]

Having a systematic process for evaluating the immigrant status of American prisoners would improve the removal of criminal aliens from the United States and make sure the most serious offenders were deported first. Law enforcement officers should prioritize the highest risk prisoners and devote their time to those cases. That will enable government authorities to use their scarce resources most effectively.

DEPOLITICIZE POLITICAL CONFLICT THROUGH AN INDEPENDENT COMMISSION

An important long-term goal in the immigration area is defusing political controversy. Long-standing concern in the general public about the number and type of people coming to America has put pressure on members of state legislatures and the U.S. Congress to adopt tough policies on immigration. Often these policies have gone too far, targeting specific nationalities for harsh, discriminatory treatment, or legislators have made decisions that are irrational from the standpoint of long-term national interests.

To defuse political contentiousness, it is time to consider the creation of an independent immigration commission. This body would have the power to interpret and implement broad congressional decisions in the same way that the Environmental Protection Agency oversees environmental policy or the Federal Communications Commission supervises telecommunications policy. Members of Congress would retain the power to set policy, but the proposed immigration commission would have the authority to administer decisionmaking.

The commission would consist of members appointed by the president and confirmed by the Senate. It would be staffed by knowledgeable experts in relevant fields, including demographers, economists, sociologists skilled in population analysis, and other social scientists with relevant skills. These researchers would study population and employment characteristics and issue periodic reports making recommendations about immigration policy. If employers had a need for more seasonal agricultural workers, skilled engineers, or other people with special talents, commission staff could document these requirements and give their expert view on what policy adjustments Congress should make.

The virtue of such a commission is that it would professionalize immigration policy. Right now, decisions are spread across an unwieldy set of legislators, legislative staff members, and agency administrators. The basis on which decisions are made is not always clear, nor do policies always closely adhere to national objectives. A more professional body charged with administering immigration policy would help create the basis for more rational policymaking.

Given the nation's history of shortsighted and problematic congressional decisions on immigration, an independent commission would shield legislators from nativist political forces and encourage calmer deliberations. Members' consistency in making poor decisions over a long period of time suggests the need for an institutional mechanism that will better serve the long-term interests of the American public.

LINK IMMIGRATION LEVELS TO THE ECONOMIC CYCLE

There clearly are challenges in elevating economic rationales in immigration policy. American support for immigration drops during recessions because native-borns fear job losses and competition over wages. During the Great Depression, for example, public concern was so strong that immigration dropped virtually to nothing. Research by writer E. J. Dionne demonstrates that citizen support for immigration drops when immigration rises and unemployment is high. Many Americans are unlikely to see a need for increased immigration when joblessness is high and economic anxiety is at a peak.[39]

Because of this connection, workforce and economic conditions should be taken into account in setting annual visa numbers. Currently, annual immigration flows continue at preset levels regardless of the employment rate or wage levels. Whether the economy is growing or not, immigration continues to flow. That lack of modulation intensifies public opposition to immigration during recessions.

A dynamic and market-based mechanism would link immigration levels to workforce needs and the shape of the overall economy. It makes sense to have policies that call for immigration to drop during recessions and rise during growth periods, or to admit more workers in particular industries when the supply of workers in those industries is inadequate. Such an approach would bolster the economy when needed at the same time it addressed public concerns by protecting native-borns from job and wage competition in difficult economic times.

Advocacy organizations understand the importance of economic cycles in shaping immigration attitudes and have endorsed such an approach. For example, Doris Meissner, a former commissioner of the U.S. Immigration and Naturalization Service and a current senior fellow at the Migration Policy Institute, has proposed that "immigration admissions levels should reflect labor market needs, employment and unemployment patterns, and shifting economic and demographic trends if immigration is to effectively contribute to the nation's longer-term growth and competitiveness needs." She argues that such a reform plan not only would help reassure Americans that they will not have to compete with immigrants for jobs during bad economic times but also that new immigrants, admitted during periods of economic growth, would find plentiful job opportunities. It makes little sense to admit "immigrants who will not fare well in the U.S. labor market" and who will suffer "long periods of unemployment and poor economic—and hence social—integration," she said. Tying immigration flows to economic conditions would help ensure that labor inflows do not "come at the expense of native workers or allow employers to avoid wage increases they would otherwise provide," she added.[40] This policy approach would address people's legitimate concerns about job competition and scarce resources and could help turn immigration into a less contentious issue.

ENCOURAGE IMMIGRANT INTEGRATION

Most new immigrants need considerable help in adapting to the United States and integrating into local communities.[41] Aid includes services such as English instruction, civic education, social services, and community activities. The U.S. Bureau of Citizenship and Immigration Services has set aside $10 million for an Immigration Integration program, $75 million for English literacy and civics education, and $730 million in Language Acquisition State Grants, among other federal programs.[42] These grants help local organizations develop in-person and online language courses and inform people about financial resources available for immigrant integration into local communities, but more money needs to be budgeted so that more immigrants can be served. For example, the quantity and quality of English classes aimed at immigrants are insufficient. Language instruction courses have long waiting lists, the quality of instruction may be low, and dropout rates are high.

U.S. Census numbers show that 21.6 million adults in the United States have limited English proficiency, although not all of these are immigrants.[43] In New York City alone, it is estimated that there are only 50,000 adult English course slots for the 1 million immigrants interested in learning the language.[44] A National

Association of Latino Elected and Appointed Officials project undertaken in 2006 found that of the 176 surveyed course providers, 57.4 percent had waiting lists ranging from "a few weeks to more than three years." Many classes were overcrowded or had students at the wrong level.[45] A 2007 study of California's adult English courses concluded that 60 percent of school districts exceeded their class enrollment caps for English instruction.[46]

This disjunction between instructional supply and demand creates problems in integrating and assimilating immigrants and leads to negative reactions for all. Native residents remain resentful when immigrants do not speak English, and immigrants are frustrated when they wait for months or years at a time for English-language instruction. The recent recession has exacerbated these tensions by reducing government funding for English courses despite increasing levels of demand.

The quality of instruction can also be problematic. Responsibility for instruction is spread among four-year colleges and universities, community colleges, elementary and secondary schools, religious organizations, libraries, community centers, and nonprofit groups. These institutions vary enormously in whether they have textbooks, employ computer-aided instruction, have language tapes, and rely on paid or volunteer instructors. Some courses are free to the pupils, while others charge thousands of dollars.

Performance outcome measures suggest these courses are not achieving their goals. For example, an analysis of Illinois English instruction courses found that 20 percent of English-as-a-second-language students drop out within four weeks of starting the class and only one-third are able to move up one level of English proficiency based on coursework.[47] A review of the literature on course effectiveness suggests considerable variation in educational quality and effective teaching across course providers.

State and federal governments provide around $1 billion annually to support adult language instructional activity, and that figure is expected to grow to $4 billion if Congress enacts a path to citizenship that mandates English mastery. But there is little oversight of the current spending and little evidence of how effective it is.[48]

The U.S. Government Accountability Office (GAO) reviewed the smorgasbord of immigration courses in 2009 and concluded that "federal support for adult English instruction is dispersed across many programs that collect little data and have limited coordination." Unlike public schools, which are required to compile extensive data on student characteristics, teacher certification, test results, graduation rates, and dropout rates, the nonprofit organizations that provide English language instruction for immigrants have very few reporting requirements, according to GAO. They may receive public money to support classes but are rarely held accountable for how they use the money or what kind of instructional results their activities produce. An analysis needs to be done of how to improve public accountability, reporting requirements, and governance and oversight in regard to public funds spent on immigrant language instruction.[49]

MODERNIZE VISA PROCESSING THROUGH DIGITAL TECHNOLOGY

The last thing required in the immigration area is a modernization of current visa application processes. Right now, the administrative system for visa processing is paper based and requires repeated mailing of applications and forms. It is a time-consuming and expensive procedure for administering entry to the United States— especially when new digital systems could offer greater efficiency and effectiveness. Currently, a long backlog of cases at the U.S. Citizenship and Immigration Services offices forces prospective immigrants to wait months or years to get visas. The human and financial cost of this system breeds disrespect for the law and encourages people to ignore the process and enter the United States illegally. A better system would use new digital technologies to allow electronic filing and processing of visa applications. Similar to the way many Americans file income tax returns, prospective immigrants could file online applications for specific visas, saving both the applicants and the government time and money.[50]

Nearly two-thirds of Americans file their tax returns online, reducing the cost and error rate of paper filing. Taxpayers who file online also receive their tax refunds more quickly. Security safeguards protect the privacy and confidentiality of taxpayer records, and citizen surveys indicate a high degree of public satisfaction with the digital experience. There is no reason that a similar system could not be developed for handling visa applications.

GUARDING AGAINST UNINTENDED CONSEQUENCES

Existing U.S. immigration policy makes little sense either from a policy or political standpoint. From a policy standpoint, the system is tilted too far in favor of family unification over other important national goals.[51] Unlike other nations, which pursue skilled workers as a matter of government policy, the U.S. system places little emphasis on economic goals or international competitiveness. Personal and humanitarian considerations have been elevated over every other possible objective.

From a political standpoint, the immigration system is controversial because the general public perceives broad costs but narrow benefits. Despite a history of immigrant "brain gains," there is little public sense that immigrants contribute much to national life. Instead, people perceive that immigrants impose huge social and economic costs. At the same time, immigrants feel aggrieved over the obstacle course of entry into the United States. In this situation, no one is very happy.

The only way to stabilize this policy area and boost public support over the long haul is to shift the visa system into better balance. Policy and politics must be realigned so that more attention is devoted to economic competitiveness, job creation, and technological innovation. If these strategic goals are emphasized, national immigration policy will pay off in a stronger economy, a more competitive country, and an American public more supportive of its new immigrants.

In making needed reforms, decisionmakers must guard against unintended policy consequences. As noted earlier the 1965 immigration reform act had the unintended consequence of boosting entry based on family ties and decreasing employment-based immigration. Occupation-linked visas went from 60 percent to 17 percent in just eight years. Lawmakers did not expect that reform bill to spark "chain immigration" in which a series of relatives brought other family members to the United States.

American policymakers must guard against a couple of risks with comprehensive reform. For example, countries that center immigration on job skills create incentives for a booming new business in fraudulent documents. In that kind of system, immigrants need credentials attesting to their educational backgrounds and personal skills. Those without proper documents may turn to firms that manufacture fake transcripts or bogus resumes. Australia, which has a job skill–based immigration policy, has experienced this problem. American legislators need to anticipate that reaction to immigration reform and take steps to minimize its occurrence through rigorous procedures for document authentication.

The other danger lies in the area of global development and foreign policy. If the United States adopts a "brain gain" policy, what happens to poor countries around the world in need of local talent? An American brain gain represents a potential brain drain for other nations. Some skeptics would argue that impoverished countries should encourage those with high-level skills and entrepreneurial drive to stay at home and help their own people advance economically and politically.

With a world population of nearly 7 billion and annual U.S. immigration of only 1 million, doubling or tripling the 65,000 high-skilled employment-related visas only means adding between

65,000 to 130,000 entrants in that category. Such a policy change would be small in the context of U.S. immigration policy and negligible from a global perspective. There are sufficient numbers of talented individuals that an immigration policy based on the Einstein principle would serve U.S. interests without endangering the development of other nations.

NOTES

CHAPTER ONE

1. Rodney Hero and Robert Preuhs, "Immigration and the Evolving American Welfare State," *American Journal of Political Science* 51 (July 2007): 498–517.

2. Donald Kinder and Cindy Kam, *Us against Them: Ethnocentric Foundations of American Opinion* (University of Chicago Press, 2009).

3. Gary Freeman, "Winners and Losers: Politics and the Costs and Benefits of Migration," in *West European Immigration and Immigrant Policy in the New Century*, edited by Anthony Messina (Westport, Conn.: Praeger, 2002).

4. Samuel Huntington, "The Hispanic Challenge," *Foreign Policy* (March/April, 2004).

5. Richard Herman and Robert Smith, *Immigrant, Inc.: Why Immigrant Entrepreneurs Are Driving the New Economy and How They Will Save the American Worker* (Hoboken, N.J.: John Wiley & Sons, 2010).

6. Thomas Friedman, "America's Real Dream Team," *New York Times*, March 21, 2010.

7. Peter Stalker, *Workers without Frontiers: The Impact of Globalization on International Migration* (London: Lynne Rienner Publishers, 2000).

8. Martin Schain, *The Politics of Immigration in France, Britain, and the United States* (New York: Palgrave Macmillan, 2008).

9. Alejandro Portes and Ruben Rumbaut, *Immigrant America* (University of California Press, 2006), p. 246.

10. Thomas Guglielmo, *White on Arrival: Italians, Race, Color, and Power in Chicago, 1890–1945* (Oxford University Press, 2003).

11. Kelly Jefferys and Randall Monger, U.S. Department of Homeland Security, Office of Immigration Statistics, *Annual Flow Report March 2008* (Government Printing Office, 2008).

12. Mae Ngai, *Impossible Subjects: Illegal Aliens and the Making of Modern America* (Princeton University Press, 2004); Rubin Martinez, *Crossing Over: A Mexican Family on the Migrant Trail* (New York: Picador, 2001).

13. Jacob Vigdor, *From Immigrants to Americans: The Rise and Fall of Fitting In* (Lanham, Md.: Rowman and Littlefield, 2010).

14. TNS Opinion, *Transatlantic Trends: Immigration* (Brussels: European Commission, 2008); Marcelo Suarez-Orozco, "Global Shifts: U.S. Immigration and the Cultural Impact of Demographic Change," Conference Series 46 (Federal Reserve Bank of Boston, June 2001).

15. Stalker, *Workers without Frontiers*.

16. TNS Opinion, *Transatlantic Trends: Immigration*.

17. Gordon Hanson, "The Economic Logic of Illegal Immigration," Council Special Report 26 (New York: Council on Foreign Relations, April, 2007), pp. 6–8.

18. Ibid.

19. Matt Richtel, "Tech Recruiting Clashes with Immigration Rules," *New York Times*, April 12, 2009.

20. Ron Hira, "H-1B Visas: It's Time for an Overhaul," *Business Week*, April 13, 2009, pp. 63–64; S. Mitra Kalita, "U.S. Deters Hiring of Foreigners as Joblessness Grows," *Wall Street Journal*, March 27, 2009.

21. Moira Herbst, "A Narrowing Window for Foreign Workers," *Business Week*, March 16, 2009, p. 50.

22. Thomas Frank, "Fewer Caught Sneaking into USA," *USA Today*, December 29, 2008, p. 1A.

23. Ibid.

24. Audrey Singer, "Twenty-First Century Gateways," in *Twenty-First Century Gateways*, edited by Singer, Hardwick, and Brettell, pp. 3–30.

25. Audrey Singer, Susan Hardwick, and Caroline Brettell, eds., *Twenty-First Century Gateways: Immigrant Incorporation in Suburban America* (Brookings, 2008).

26. Demetrios Papademetriou and Aaron Terrazas, "Immigrants and the Current Economic Crisis" (Washington: Migration Policy Institute, January 2009).

27. Thomas MaCurdy, Thomas Nechyba, and Jay Bhattacharya, "An Economic Framework for Assessing the Fiscal Impacts of Immigration," in *The Immigration Debate: Studies on the Economic, Demographic,*

and Fiscal Effects of Immigration, edited by James P. Smith and Barry Edmonston (Washington: National Academy Press, 1998).

28. TNS Opinion, *Transatlantic Trends: Immigration*.

29. Ronald Lee and Timothy Miller, "The Current Fiscal Impact of Immigrants and Their Descendants: Beyond the Immigrant Household," in *The Immigration Debate*, edited by Smith and Edmonston.

30. Immigration Policy Center, "Economic Growth and Immigration: Bridging the Demographic Divide" (Washington: American Immigration Council, formerly American Immigration Law Foundation, November 2005), p. 8.

31. James P. Smith and Barry Edmonston, eds., *The New Americans: Economic, Demographic, and Fiscal Effects of Immigration* (Washington: National Research Council, National Academy of Sciences Press, 1997), pp. 220, 353.

32. Gary Painter and Zhou Yu, "Leaving Gateway Metropolitan Areas in the United States: Immigrants and the Housing Market," *Urban Studies* 45 (May 2008): 1163–91.

33. Emily Bazar, "Most Illegal Immigrants' Kids Legal," *USA Today*, April 15, 2009, p. 3A.

34. Ceci Connolly, "Senate Passes Health Insurance Bill for Children," *Washington Post*, January 30, 2009, p. A1.

35. Abby Goodnough, "Massachusetts Takes a Step Back from Health Care for All," *New York Times*, July 15, 2009.

36. N. C. Aizenam, "Illegal Immigrants in Md. and Va. Out-Earn U.S. Peers," *Washington Post*, November 29, 2007, p. A10.

37. Alexander N. Ortega and others, "Health Care Access, Use of Services, and Experiences among Undocumented Mexicans and Other Latinos," *Archives of Internal Medicine* 167 (November 26, 2007): 2354–60.

38. Stephen Moore, *A Fiscal Portrait of the Newest Americans* (Washington: National Immigration Forum and Cato Institute, 1998).

39. Smith and Edmonston, eds., *The New Americans*, pp. 220, 353.

40. White House, *Economic Report of the President* (GPO, February 2005), p. 107.

41. White House, Council of Economic Advisers, *Immigration's Economic Impact* (GPO, June 20, 2007), p. 3.

42. Philip Martin and Elizabeth Midgley, "Immigration: Shaping and Reshaping America," *Population Bulletin* 61 (Washington: Population Reference Bureau, December 2006).

43. Giovanni Peri, "Rethinking the Effects of Immigration on Wages" (Washington: American Immigration Council, Immigration Policy Center, October 2006), p. 2. Also see George Borjas, *Friends or Strangers: The Impact of Immigrants on the U.S. Economy* (New York: Basic Books, 1990).

44. Peri, "Rethinking the Effects of Immigration on Wages," p. 2.

45. U.S. Bureau of Labor Statistics, "Foreign-Born Workers: Labor Force Characteristics in 2008" (March 26, 2009).

46. Hanson, "The Economic Logic of Illegal Immigration," pp. 16–18.

47. E. J. Dionne Jr., "Democracy in the Age of New Media: A Report on the Media and the Immigration Debate" (Brookings, 2008).

48. Vivek Wadhwa, Ben Rissing, AnnaLee Saxenian, and Gary Gereffi, "America's New Immigrant Entrepreneurs," Report by Duke School of Engineering and the University of California Berkeley School of Information (January 4, 2007).

49. Ibid.

50. Vivek Wadhwa, Ben Rissing, AnnaLee Saxenian, and Gary Gereffi, "Education, Entrepreneurship and Immigration," Report by Duke School of Engineering and the University of California Berkeley School of Information (June 11, 2007).

51. Gnanaraj Chellaraj, Keith Maskus, and Aaditya Mattoo, "The Contribution of Skilled Immigration and International Graduate Students to U.S. Innovation" Policy Research Working Paper 3588 (Washington: World Bank, May 2005).

52. Robert Fairlie, "Kauffman Index of Entrepreneurial Activity, 1996–2008" (University of California at Santa Cruz, April 2009).

53. AnnaLee Saxenian, *The Role of Immigrant Entrepreneurs in New Venture Creation* (Stanford University Press, 2001).

54. AnnaLee Saxenian, "Silicon Valley's New Immigrant Entrepreneurs" (San Francisco: Public Policy Institute of California, 1999), pp. 9–13.

55. Chellaraj, Maskus, and Mattoo, "The Contribution of Skilled Immigration and International Graduate Students to U.S. Innovation."

56. TNS Opinion, *Transatlantic Trends: Immigration*.

57. *The Economist*, "Enlightenment Man," December 4, 2008.

58. Academy of Achievement, "Biography of Pierre Omidyar" (www.achievement.org [March 25, 2009]).

59. Richard Tedlow, *Andy Grove: The Life and Times of an American* (New York: Penguin Books, 2006).

60. Paul Kupperberg, *Jerry Yang* (New York: Chelsea House Publishers, 2009).

61. Herman and Smith, *Immigrant, Inc.*

62. Gianmarco Ottaviano and Giovanni Peri, "The Economic Value of Cultural Diversity: Evidence from U.S. Cities," *Journal of Economic Geography* 6 (2006): 9–44.

63. Richard Florida, *The Rise of the Creative Class* (New York: Basic Books, 2002).

64. Gallup Poll, "Americans Have Become More Negative on Impact of Immigrants" (Washington: June 4–24, 2007) (www.gallup.com).

65. Charles Hirschman, "Immigration and the American Century," *Demography* 42 (November 2005): 610.

66. George Will, "Clemente," *New York Times Book Review*, May 7, 2006, p. 13.

67. Vartan Gregorian, *The Road to Home: My Life and Times* (New York: Simon and Schuster, 2003).

68. Madeleine Albright, *Madam Secretary* (New York: Miramax Books, 2003).

69. Wadhwa and others, "America's New Immigrant Entrepreneurs."

CHAPTER TWO

1. John Torpey, *The Invention of the Passport* (Cambridge University Press, 2000).

2. Gerald Neuman, *Strangers to the Constitution: Immigrants, Borders, and Fundamental Law* (Princeton University Press, 1996).

3. Janie Lorber, *New York Times,* "U.S. Bares 'Alien Files' Kept on Immigrants," August 11, 2009.

4. Geoffrey Sayre-McCord, ed., *Crime and Family* (Temple University Press, 2007).

5. Vivek Wadhwa, Ben Rissing, AnnaLee Saxenian, and Gary Gereffi, "America's New Immigrant Entrepreneurs," Report by the Duke School of Engineering and the University of California Berkeley School of Information (January 4, 2007).

6. Neuman, *Strangers to the Constitution.*

7. Matthew Spalding, "From Pluribus to Unum: Immigration and the Founding Fathers," *Policy Review* no. 67 (1994): 35–41.

8. Neuman, *Strangers to the Constitution.*

9. Harold M. Hyman, *American Singularity: The 1787 Northwest Ordinance, the 1862 Homestead and Morrill Acts, and the 1944 G.I. Bill* (University of Georgia Press, 1986).

10. D. C. Corbett, "Immigration and Economic Development," *Canadian Journal of Economics and Political Science* 27 (August 1951): 360–68; Thomas Weiss and Donald Schaefer, eds., *American Economic Development in Historical Perspective* (Stanford University Press, 1994).

11. Daniel Tichenor, *Dividing Line: The Politics of Immigration Control in America* (Princeton University Press, 2002).

12. John Higham, *Strangers in the Land: Patterns of American Nativism, 1860–1925* (Rutgers University Press, 1988).

13. Martin Schain, *The Politics of Immigration in France, Britain, and the United States* (New York: Palgrave Macmillan, 2008), pp. 191–92.

14. Tichenor, *Dividing Line.*

15. James Gimpel and James Edwards Jr., *The Congressional Politics of Immigration Reform* (Boston: Allyn and Bacon, 1999).

16. Wikipedia, "History of Laws Concerning Immigration and Naturalization in the United States" (http://en.wikipedia.org/wiki/History_of_laws_concerning_immigration_and_naturalization_in_the_United_States [May 20, 2009]).

17. Ibid.

18. Wendy Ng, *Japanese American Internment during World War II* (Westport, Conn.: Greenwood, 2002).

19. Cheryl Shanks, *Immigration and the Politics of American Sovereignty, 1890–1990* (University of Michigan Press, 2001).

20. Robert Desmond, *Tides of War* (University of Iowa Press, 1984), p. 448.

21. Percentage cited at www.cis.org/articles/1995/back395.html.

22. Schain, *The Politics of Immigration in France, Britain, and the United States*, p. 199.

23. Emanuel Celler, speech, *Congressional Record*, August 25, 1965, p. 21812.

24. Robert Kennedy, Letter to the Editor, *New York Times*, August 24, 1964, p. 26.

25. Schain, *The Politics of Immigration in France, Britain, and the United States*, p. 269.

26. Edward Kennedy, speech (www.cis.org/articles/1995/back395.html).

27. Celler, *Congressional Record*.

28. Lyndon Johnson, *Public Papers of the Presidents of the United States* (Government Printing Office, 1966), pp. 1037–40.

29. Jay Belsky, "Parental and Non-Parental Child Care and Children's Socio-Emotional Development," *Journal of Marriage and the Family* 52, no. 4 (1990): 885–903; Matthew Bumpus, Ann Crouter, and S. McHale, "Work Demands of Dual-Earner Couples: Implications for Parents' Knowledge about Children's Daily Lives in Middle Childhood," *Journal of Marriage and Family* 61 (1999): 465–75; Toby Parcel and Elizabeth Menaghan, "Early Parental Work, Family Social Capital, and Early Childhood Outcomes," *American Journal of Sociology* 99 (1994): 972–1009; and Thomas Vander Ven, *Working Mothers and Juvenile Delinquency* (New York: LFB Scholarly Publishing, 2003).

30. Sayre-McCord, ed., *Crime and Family*.

31. Michael Wadsworth, *Roots of Delinquency: Infancy, Adolescence, and Crime* (New York: Barnes and Noble Books, 1979), p. 115.

32. Jackson Toby, "The Differential Impact of Family Disorganization," *American Sociological Review* 22 (October 1957): 512.

33. Hugh Davis Graham, *Collision Course: The Strange Convergence of Affirmative Action and Immigration Policy in America* (Oxford University Press, 2002, pp. 102–03).

34. David Stoll, "In Focus: The Immigration Debate." Project of the Institute for Policy Studies and the Interhemispheric Resource Center, Silver City, N.M. (www.theodora.com/debate.html), undated.

35. Randall Monger and Nancy Rytina, "U.S. Legal Permanent Residents: 2008," *Annual Flow Report* (U.S. Department of Homeland Security, March, 2009), p. 3.

36. Richard Freeman, Emily Jin, and Chia-Yu Shen, "Where Do New U.S.-Trained Science-Engineering PhDs Come From?" NBER Working Paper W10554 (Cambridge, Mass.: National Bureau of Economic Research, June 2004).

37. Teresa Bevis and Christopher Lucas, *International Students in American Colleges and Universities* (New York: Palgrave Macmillan, 2007).

38. Ron Hira, "H-1B Visas: It's Time for an Overhaul," *Business Week,* April 13, 2009, pp. 63–64.

39. Global Workers Justice Alliance, "Migration Data and Labor Rights," undated (www.globalworkers.org/migrationdata_mx.html).

40. Gordon Hanson, "The Economic Logic of Illegal Immigration," Council Special Report 26 (New York: Council on Foreign Relations, April 2007), pp. 6–8.

41. Toby, "The Differential Impact of Family Disorganization," p. 512.

42. Wadsworth, *Roots of Delinquency,* p. 115.

43. Scott Keeter, "Where the Public Stands on Immigration Reform" (Washington: Pew Research Center, November 23, 2009).

44. U.S. Border Patrol budget (www.data360.org/dsg.aspx?Data_Set_Group_Id=1484).

CHAPTER THREE

1. Brian Massumi, ed., *The Politics of Everyday Fear* (University of Minnesota Press, 1993).

2. Donald Kinder and Cindy Kam, *Us against Them: Ethnocentric Foundations of American Opinion* (University of Chicago Press, 2009).

3. Frank Baumgartner and Bryan Jones, *Agenda and Instability in American Politics,* 2d ed. (University of Chicago Press, 2009).

4. Daniel Tichenor, *Dividing Lines: The Politics of Immigration Control in America* (Princeton University Press, 2002).

5. Ralph Ketcham, *James Madison* (New York: Macmillan, 1971); Gary Mucciaroni and Paul Quirk, *Deliberative Choices: Debating Public Policy in Congress* (University of Chicago Press, 2006).

6. Tom Mann and Norman Ornstein, *The Broken Branch: How Congress Is Failing America and How to Get It Back on Track* (Oxford University Press, 2008).

7. David Mayhew, *Divided We Govern* (Yale University Press, 1991).

8. Pietro Nivola and David Brady, eds., *Red and Blue Nation? Characteristics and Causes of America's Polarized Politics* (Brookings, 2006).

9. Theodore Lowi, *The End of Liberalism*, 2d ed. (New York: W. W. Norton, 1979).

10. Paul Light, *A Government Ill Executed: The Decline of Federal Service and How to Reverse It* (Harvard University Press, 2008).

11. John Kingdon, *Agendas, Alternatives, and Public Policies* (New York: Longman, 2003).

12. Baumgartner and Jones, *Agendas and Instability in American Politics*.

13. Martin West and Paul Peterson, eds., *School Money Trials: The Legal Pursuit of Education Adequacy* (Brookings, 2007).

14. Wendy Schiller, *Partners and Rivals: Representation in U.S. Senate Delegations* (Princeton University Press, 2000); Eric Patashnik, *Reforms at Risk: What Happens after Major Policy Changes Are Enacted* (Princeton University Press, 2008).

15. James Gimpel and James Edwards Jr., *The Congressional Politics of Immigration Reform* (Boston: Allyn and Bacon, 1999).

16. Cheryl Shanks, *Immigration and the Politics of American Sovereignty, 1890–1990* (University of Michigan Press, 2001).

17. Tichenor, *Dividing Lines*.

18. A. A. Gray, *History of California* (New York: D.C. Heath, 1934).

19. *Illustrated Wasp*, untitled article, August 12, 1882.

20. *Harper's Weekly*, "The Heathen Chinese," 15 (1871).

21. *San Francisco Wave*, "Raids on Chinese," November 15, 1890, p. 1.

22. David Wright-Neville and Debra Smith, "Political Rage: Terrorism and the Politics of Emotion," *Global Change, Reason, and Society* 21 (Fall 2009): 85–98.

23. Caryl Rivers, *Selling Anxiety* (Hanover, N.H.: University Press of New England, 2007).

24. Matthew Brezezinski, "Hady Hassan Omar's Detention," *New York Times Magazine*, October 27, 2002.

25. Rachel Ida Buff, "The Deportation Terror," *American Quarterly* (September, 2008): 523–51.

26. *Ethiopian Review*, "Bloomberg on Immigration Policy," January 4, 2010.

27. Glenn Greenwald, *How Would a Patriot Act?* (San Francisco: Working Assets, 2006).

28. Deb Riechmann, "Bush Says Immigration Reform Key to Relations with Latin America," *Seattle Times*, March 14, 2007.

29. Darrell West and Thomas Mann, "Prospects for Immigration Reform in the New Political Climate," Paper (Brookings, July 2009).

30. Walter Shapiro, "Another Bush, Another Push for Immigration Reform," *Politics Daily*, July 9, 2009.

31. Bill Walsh and Colley Charpentier, "Vitter Leads Opposition to Immigration Bill," *New Orleans Times-Picayune*, June 22, 2007.

32. E. J. Dionne, "A Report on the Media and the Immigration Debate" (Brookings, 2008), p. 6.

33. Randal Archibold, "Arizona Enacts Stringent Law on Immigration," *New York Times*, April 23, 2010.

34. Randal Archibold and Megan Thee-Brenan, "Poll Shows Most in U.S. Want Overhaul of Immigration Laws," *New York Times*, May 3, 2010.

35. William Rashbaum, Mark Mazzetti, and Peter Baker, "Arrest Made in Times Square Bomb Case," *New York Times*, May 4, 2010.

36. Mucciaroni and Quirk, *Deliberative Choices*.

37. Migration Policy Institute, "Testimony of Doris Meissner," Congressional hearing on comprehensive immigration reform (Washington, April 30, 2009).

38. Brookings-Duke Immigration Policy Roundtable, "Breaking the Immigration Stalemate: From Deep Disagreements to Constructive Proposals," Paper (Brookings, September 2009).

39. Sheila Jasanoff, *The Fifth Branch: Science Advisors as Policy-Makers* (Harvard University Press, 1990).

CHAPTER FOUR

1. Marion Just, Ann Crigler, Timothy Cook, Dean Alger, Montague Kern, and Darrell West, *Cross Talk* (University of Chicago Press, 1996).

2. Thomas Patterson, *Out of Order* (New York: Vintage, 1994).

3. Daphne Eviatar, "Nightly Nativism," *Nation*, August 28, 2006.

4. Kamla Pande, "The Effect of September 11, 2001, on Media Discourse and Public Opinion toward Immigration," senior honors thesis, University of Michigan, 2006. Results cited by Ted Brader, Nicholas Valentino, and Elizabeth Suhay, "What Triggers Public Opposition to Immigration? Anxiety, Group Cues, and Immigration Threat," *American Journal of Political Science* 52 (October 2008): 959–78.

5. Leo Ralph Chavez, *Covering Immigration* (University of California Press, 2001).

6. Darrell West, *The Rise and Fall of the Media Establishment* (Boston: Bedford/St. Martins Press, 2001).

7. William McGowan, *Coloring the News: How Crusading for Diversity Has Corrupted American Journalism* (San Francisco: Encounter Books, 2001).

8. *Harper's Weekly*, "Who May Be Citizens of the United States?" 2 (1857).

9. *Harper's* Weekly, "Affairs in China," 4 (1860).

10. *Harper's Weekly*, "Chinese Reasoning," 9 (1865).

11. *Harper's Weekly*, "Chinese Immigration," 20 (1876).

12. *Harper's Weekly*, "Chinese in America," 21 (1877).

13. *Illustrated Wasp*, "The Chinese Must Go," May 11, 1878.

14. *Illustrated Wasp*, "Uncle Sam's Farm in Danger," March 9, 1878.

15. *Illustrated Wasp*, "The Dens of Chinatown," 1880.

16. *Harper's Weekly*, "The Chinese Exclusion Bill," April 16, 1892, p. 362.

17. *San Francisco Wave*, "Senseless Prejudice" (Jan.-June 1892): 5.

18. Francis A. Walker, "Restriction of Immigration," *Atlantic Monthly* 77 (June 1896): 822–29.

19. William Ripley, "Races in the United States," *Atlantic Monthly* (December 1908).

20. Randolph Bourne, "Trans-National America," *Atlantic Monthly* (July 1916).

21. Don Lescohier, "Immigration and the Labor-Supply," *Atlantic Monthly* (April 1919).

22. "No Irish Need Apply" (www.rifuture.org [January 14, 2009]).

23. *Harper's Weekly*, "Poor House from Galway," undated.

24. "American Gold" (www.hsp.org [April 13, 2009]).

25. "Uncle Sam's Lodging-House" (www.hsp.org [April 13, 2009]).

26. *Harper's Weekly*, "The Threat of Immigration to American Culture," August 30, 1873.

27. "The Irish as Unmixable in the National Pot," reprinted in *The American Heritage History of the American People*, edited by Bernard Weisberger (New York: HarperCollins 1971), p. 175.

28. Michelle Marie Cobas, "Mass Media Ethics vs. Ethnic Identity: The Cuban American National Foundation's Battle with the *Miami Herald*," thesis submitted to the graduate faculty of the Louisiana State University, 2001.

29. Richard Woodbury and George Church, "The Welcome Wears Thin," *Time*, September 1, 1980.

30. *Time*, "Start of a New Exodus," April 28, 1980.

31. *Time*, "Trouble in Paradise," November 23, 1981.

32. *Time*, "Controls for an Alien Invasion," August 3, 1981.

33. Cathy Booth, "Send 'Em Back!" *Time*, June 8, 1992.

34. Christine Gorman and Cathy Booth, "Opening the Border to AIDS," *Time*, February 22, 1993.

35. Joel Millman, "Going Nativist," *Columbia Journalism Review* 37 (January/February 1999): 60–65.

36. Cort Kirkwood, "A Resurgence of Deadly Diseases," *The New American*, November 27, 2006.

37. National Association of Hispanic Journalists, "NAHJ Calls for Truth and Fairness in Swine Flu Coverage," undated press release, 2009.

38. Sara McElmurry, "Elvira Arellano: No Rosa Parks: Creation of 'Us' versus 'Them' in an Opinion Column," *Hispanic Journal of Behavioral Sciences* 31 (February 10, 2009): 182.

39. Mary Mitchell, "Immigrant Activist Holed Up in Church Is No Rosa Parks," *Chicago Sun-Times*, August 22, 2006.

40. Anne Teresa Demo, "The After-Image: Immigration Policy after Elian," *Rhetoric and Public Affairs* 10 (Spring 2007): 27–50.

41. Manoucheka Celeste, "Media Portrayals of Cubans and Haitians: A Comparative Study of the *New York Times*," thesis presented to the graduate school of the University of Florida, 2005.

42. Darrell West, "The New Digital Press: How to Create a Brighter Future for the News Industry," Issues in Governance Studies (Brookings Institution, May 2009).

43. Richard Perez-Pena, "As Cities Go from Two Papers to One, Talk of Zero," *New York Times*, March 12, 2009.

44. Pew Research Center Project for Excellence in Journalism, "The State of the News Media 2009" (www.stateofthemedia.org/2009/index.htm).

45. Paul Farhi, "NPR Achieves Record Ratings," *Washington Post*, March 24, 2009, p. C1.

46. Bruce Bimber, *Information and American Democracy* (Cambridge University Press, 2003).

47. Diana Owen and Richard Davis, *New Media and American Politics* (Oxford University Press, 1998).

48. Darrell West, "The Two Faces of Twitter: Revolution in a Digital Age for Iran," *Huffington Post*, June 22, 2009.

49. Kathleen Hall Jamieson and Paul Waldman, *The Press Effect: Politicians, Journalists, and the Stories That Shape the Political World* (Oxford University Press, 2004).

50. Leslie Savan, "Anti-Mexican Media Hysteria Makes Life More Dangerous for Latinos in the U.S.," *Nation*, May 13, 2009.

51. Media Matters for America, "Paranoia Pandemic: Conservative Media Baselessly Blame Swine Flu Outbreak on Immigrants," press release, April 27, 2009.

52. Robert Suro, "A Report on the Media and the Immigration Debate" (Brookings Institution, 2008), p. 52.

53. Ibid., p. 25.

54. Ibid., pp. 71–72.

55. Ibid., p. 83.

56. Ibid., p. 83.

57. Owen and Davis, *New Media and American Politics*.

58. Jamieson and Waldman, *The Press Effect: Politicians, Journalists, and the Stories That Shape the Political World.*

59. Pande, "The Effect of September 11, 2001, on Media Discourse and Public Opinion toward Immigration."

60. Vivek Wadhwa, Ben Rissing, AnnaLee Saxenian, and Gary Gereffi, "America's New Immigrant Entrepreneurs," Report by the Duke School of Engineering and the University of California Berkeley School of Information (January 4, 2007).

61. West, "The New Digital Press."

62. West, *The Rise and Fall of the Media Establishment.*

63. Sam Roberts, "In a Generation, Minorities May Be the U.S. Majority," *New York Times*, August 13, 2008.

64. Roger Lowenstein, "The Immigration Equation," *New York Times Magazine*, July 9, 2006.

CHAPTER FIVE

1. Russell Neuman, George Marcus, Michael MacKuen, and Ann Crigler, eds., *The Affect Effect: Dynamics of Emotion in Political Thinking and Behavior* (University of Chicago Press, 2007); George Marcus, John Sullivan, Elizabeth Theiss-Morse, and Daniel Stevens, "The Emotional Foundations of Political Cognition," *Political Psychology* 26, no. 6 (2005): 949–63.

2. David Sears and Jack Citrin, *Tax Revolt: Something for Nothing in California* (Harvard University Press, 1982).

3. Tali Mendelberg, *The Race Card: Campaign Strategy, Implicit Message, and the Norm of Equality* (Princeton University Press, 2001).

4. Donald Kinder and Cindy Kam, *Us against Them: Ethnocentric Foundations of American Opinion* (University of Chicago Press, 2009).

5. Paul Kellstedt, *The Mass Media and the Dynamics of American Racial Attitudes* (Cambridge University Press, 2003).

6. Ted Brader, "Striking a Responsive Chord: How Political Ads Motivate and Persuade Voters by Appealing to Emotions," *American Journal of Political Science* 49 (April 2005): 388–405. See also his book, *Campaigning for Hearts and Minds* (University of Chicago Press, 2006), and Donald Kinder and Lynn Sanders, *Divided by Color: Racial Politics and Democratic Ideals* (University of Chicago Press, 1996).

7. James Stimson, *Public Opinion in America: Moods, Cycles, and Swings*, 2d ed. (Boulder, Colo.: Westview Press, 1999).

8. Benjamin Page and Robert Shapiro, *The Rational Public* (University of Chicago Press, 1992).

9. Denis Sullivan and Roger Masters, "Happy Warriors: Leaders' Facial Displays, Viewers' Emotions and Political Support," *American Journal of Political Science* 32, no. 2 (1988): 345–68.

10. Ted Brader, Nicholas Valentino, and Elizabeth Suhay, "What Triggers Public Opposition to Immigration? Anxiety, Group Cues, and Immigration Threat," *American Journal of Political Science* 52 (October 2008): 959–78.

11. Rodney Hero and Robert Preuhs, "Immigration and the Evolving American Welfare State," *American Journal of Political Science* 51 (July 2007): 498–517.

12. Thomas Frank, "Fewer Caught Sneaking into USA," *USA Today*, December 29, 2008, p. 1A.

13. Daniel Tichenor, *Dividing Line: The Politics of Immigration Control in America* (Princeton University Press, 2002).

14. Leonie Huddy, Stanley Feldman, and Erin Cassese, "On the Distinct Political Effects of Anxiety and Anger," in *The Affect Effect*, edited by Neuman and others, pp. 202–30.

15. Benjamin Woods Labaree, *The Boston Tea Party* (Northeastern University Press, 1979).

16. Leonard Richards, *Shays' Rebellion: The American Revolution's Final Battle* (University of Pennsylvania Press, 2002).

17. Darrell M. West, *The Rise and Fall of the Media Establishment* (Boston: Bedford/St. Martin's Press, 2001), pp. 38–41.

18. Kenneth Stampp, *The Era of Reconstruction, 1865–1877* (New York: Knopf, 1966), p. 167.

19. William Gillette, *Retreat from Reconstruction 1869–1879* (Louisiana State University Press, 1979).

20. Stewart Tolnay and E. M. Beck, *A Festival of Violence: An Analysis of Southern Lynching, 1882–1930* (University of Illinois Press, 1995).

21. Joan Crouse, *The Homeless Transient in the Great Depression* (State University of New York Press, 1986).

22. T. Harry Williams, *Huey Long* (New York: Vintage Press, 1981).

23. Sears and Citrin, *Tax Revolt: Something for Nothing in California*; Howard Jarvis and Robert Pack, *I'm Mad as Hell: The Exclusive Story of the Tax Revolt and Its Leader* (New York: Times Books, 1979).

24. Bill Piper, "A Brief Analysis of Voter Behavior Regarding Tax Initiatives, from 1978 to 1999." (Initiative and Referendum Institute, University of Southern California 2001) (www.iandrinstitute.org/indepth/piper.htm).

25. Jeff Zeleny, "Thousands Rally in Capital to Protest Big Government," *New York Times*, September 12, 2009.

26. Brader, Valentino, and Suhay, "What Triggers Public Opposition to Immigration?"

27. Antoine Banks, "Affirmative Action and Immigration: Anger's Ability to Prime Whites' Racial Attitudes," Paper presented at the annual meeting of the International Society of Political Psychology, Sciences Program, Paris, May 23, 2009.

28. Rasmussen Reports, "32% Angry about Immigration, but Not Mad at Immigrants" (Asbury Park, N.J.: June 12, 2008).

29. Joel Fetzer, *Public Attitudes toward Immigration in the United States, France, and Germany* (Cambridge University Press, 2000).

30. Rasmussen Reports, "32% Angry about Immigration, but Not Mad at Immigrants."

31. Patrick McDonnell, "Prop. 187 Found Unconstitutional by Federal Judge," *Los Angeles Times*, November 15, 1997.

32. Irwin Morris, "African American Voting on Proposition 187," *Political Research Quarterly* 53, no. 1 (2000): 77–98.

33. *Economist*, "Heading North: After Proposition 187," November 19, 1994.

34. Jack Citrin, Donald Green, Christopher Muste, and Cara Wong, "Public Opinion toward Immigration Reform: The Role of Economic Motivations," *Journal of Politics* 59, no. 3 (1997): 858–81.

35. Diane Mackie and Eliot Smith, *From Prejudice to Intergroup Emotions* (New York: Psychology Press, 2003).

36. Brader, Valentino, and Suhay, "What Triggers Public Opposition to Immigration?"

37. Paul Sniderman, Louk Hagendoorn, and Markus Prior, "Predispositional Factors and Situational Triggers: Exclusionary Reactions to Immigrant Minorities," *American Political Science Review* 98, no. 1 (2004): 35–50.

38. John Lapinski, Pia Peltola, Greg Shaw, and Alan Yang, "The Polls—Trends: Immigrants and Immigration," *Public Opinion Quarterly* 62, no. 2 (1997): 356–83.

39. James Gimpel and James Edwards Jr., *The Congressional Politics of Immigration Reform* (Boston: Allyn and Bacon, 1999).

40. Martin Schain, *The Politics of Immigration in France, Britain, and the United States* (New York: Palgrave Macmillan, 2008).

41. Cathy Booth, "Send 'Em Back!" *Time*, June 8, 1992; Christine Gorman and Cathy Booth, "Opening the Border to AIDS," *Time*, February 22, 1993.

42. Lymari Morales, "Americans Return to Tougher Immigration Stance" (Washington: Gallup Poll, August 5, 2009) (www.gallup.com).

43. E. J. Dionne Jr., "Democracy in the Age of New Media: A Report on the Media and the Immigration Debate" (Brookings, 2008).

44. Morales, "Americans Return to Tougher Immigration Stance."

45. Dionne, "Democracy in the Age of New Media."

46. Rita Simon and James Lynch, "A Comparative Assessment of Public Opinion toward Immigrants and Immigration Practices," *International Migration Review* 33, no. 2 (1999): 455–67.

47. Frank Baumgartner and Bryan Jones, *Agenda and Instability in American Politics,* 2d ed. (University of Chicago Press, 2009).

48. Pew Research Center for the People and the Press, "Economy, Jobs Trump All Other Policy Priorities in 2009" (Washington: January 22, 2009) (http://people-press.org).

49. Jeffrey Jones, "Fewer Americans Favor Cutting Back Immigration," (Washington: Gallup Poll, July 10, 2008), (www.gallup.com).

50. Dionne, "Democracy in the Age of New Media," p. 80.

51. Pew Research Center for the People and the Press, "Trends in Political Values and Core Attitudes: 1987–2009" (Washington: May 21, 2009), p. 65.

52. Gallup Poll, "Bush's Speech on Immigration Closely Follows Public Opinion" (Washington: May 17, 2006) (www.gallup.com).

53. Gimpel and Edwards, *The Congressional Politics of Immigration Reform.*

54. Joseph Nye Jr., Philip Zelikow, and David King, eds., *Why People Don't Trust Government* (Harvard University Press, 1997).

CHAPTER SIX

1. James Q. Wilson, *Bureaucracy: What Government Agencies Do and Why They Do It* (New York: Basic Books, 1991).

2. Michael Lipsky, *Street-Level Bureaucrats* (New York: Russell Sage Foundation, 1983).

3. Jeffrey Pressman and Aaron Wildavsky, *Implementation: How Great Expectations in Washington Are Decided in Oakland* (University of California Press, 1984).

4. Wilson, *Bureaucracy: What Government Agencies Do and Why They Do It.*

5. Martha Derthick and Paul Quirk, *The Politics of Deregulation* (Brookings, 1985).

6. Leo Ralph Chavez, *Covering Immigration* (University of California Press, 2001).

7. Associated Press, "Texas Using Web Cameras on Mexican Border," November 3, 2006.

8. U.S. Customs and Border Patrol, "2008 Fiscal Year in Review," (2009).

9. U.S. Customs and Immigration Service, "Annual Report for Fiscal Year 2008" (August 1, 2009).

10. Russell Wheeler, "Seeking Fair and Effective Administration of Immigration Laws," Policy report (Brookings, July 2009).

11. AILA InfoNet Document 09050766, "A New Era of Responsibility: President Obama's Fiscal 2010 Budget" (Washington: American Immigration Lawyers Association, May 7, 2009).

12. Pew Research Center for the People and the Press, "Trends in Political Values and Core Attitudes: 1987–2009" (Washington: May 21, 2009), p. 65.

13. Thomas Frank, "Fewer Caught Sneaking into USA," *USA Today*, December 29, 2008, p. 1A.

14. Ibid.

15. Julia Preston, "Mexican Data Say Migration to U.S. Has Plummeted," *New York Times*, May 15, 2009.

16. Frank, "Fewer Caught Sneaking into USA."

17. Marshall Fitz and Angela Kelley, "Principles for Immigration Reform" (Washington: Center for American Progress, December 2009), p. 6.

18. Tyche Hendricks, "Study: Price for Border Fence Up to $49 Billion," *San Francisco Chronicle*, January 8, 2007.

19. Ibid.

20. Ginger Thompson, "Work under Way on 'Virtual Fence,'" *New York Times*, May 8, 2009.

21. Spencer Hsu, "Work to Cease on 'Virtual Fence" along U.S.-Mexico Border," *Washington Post*, March 16, 2010.

22. Pew Research Center for the People and the Press, "Trends in Political Values and Core Attitudes," p. 65.

23. Spencer Hsu, "Little New in Obama's Immigration Policy," *Washington Post*, May 20, 2009.

24. Associated Press, "Texas Using Web Cameras on Mexican Border."

25. Ibid.

26. Kenneth Stampp, *The Era of Reconstruction, 1865–1877* (New York: Knopf, 1966), p. 167.

27. Spencer Hsu, "Hate Crimes Rise as Immigration Debate Heats Up," *Washington Post*, June 16, 2009.

28. Ibid.

29. J. Ramji-Nogales, A. Schoenholtz, and P. Shrag, "Refugee Roulette: Disparities in Asylum Adjudication," *Stanford Law Review* 60 (2007): 338.

30. Nina Bernstein, "In City of Lawyers, Many Immigrants Fighting Deportation Go It Alone," *New York Times*, March 13, 2009.

31. Syracuse University TRAC Immigration, "Case Backlogs in Immigration Courts Expand, Resulting Wait Times Grow" (2009).

32. Mark Hamblett, "Lawyers Target 'Assembly Line' Practice, Abuse of Poor Immigrants," *New York Law Journal*, January 4, 2010.

33. Syracuse University TRAC Immigration, "Case Backlogs in Immigration Courts Expand, Resulting Wait Times Grow."

34. N. C. Aizenman, "Backlog of Hearings at All-Time High in U.S. Immigration Courts," *Washington Post*, March 12, 2010.

35. Wheeler, "Seeking Fair and Effective Administration of Immigration Laws."

36. John Schwartz, "Immigration Enforcement Fuels Spike in U.S. Cases," *New York Times*, December 21, 2009.

37. Julia Preston, "Immigration Judges Found under Strain," *New York Times*, July 10, 2009.

38. Ramji-Nogales, Schoenholtz, and Shrag, "Refugee Roulette: Disparities in Asylum Adjudication."

39. Wheeler, "Seeking Fair and Effective Administration of Immigration Laws."

40. Ibid.

41. Michael Falcone, "100,000 Parents of Citizens Were Deported over 10 Years," *New York Times*, February 14, 2009.

42. Martin Schain, *The Politics of Immigration in France, Britain, and the United States* (New York: Palgrave Macmillan, 2008).

43. Rodney Hero and Robert Preuhs, "Immigration and the Evolving American Welfare State," *American Journal of Political Science* 51 (July 2007): 498–517.

44. Pew Hispanic Center, "A Portrait of Unauthorized Immigrants in the United States" (Washington: April 14, 2009).

45. Wheeler, "Seeking Fair and Effective Administration of Immigration Laws."

46. U.S. Immigration and Customs Enforcement, "Worksite Enforcement Overview" (April 30, 2009).

47. Wheeler, "Seeking Fair and Effective Administration of Immigration Laws."

48. N. C. Aizenman, "Conflicting Accounts of an ICE Raid in Md.," *Washington Post*, February 18, 2009, p. A1.

49. Spencer Hsu, "Delay in Immigration Raids May Signal Policy Change," *Washington Post*, March 29, 2009, p. A2.

50. Julia Preston, "U.S. Shifts Strategy on Illicit Work by Immigrants," *New York Times*, July 3, 2009.

51. Spencer Hsu, "U.S. to Expand Immigration Checks to All Local Jails," *Washington Post*, May 19, 2009.

52. Pew Research Center for the People and the Press, "Trends in Political Values and Core Attitudes," p. 65.

CHAPTER SEVEN

1. Randall Monger and Nancy Rytina, "U.S. Legal Permanent Residents: 2008," *Annual Flow Report* (U.S. Department of Homeland Security, March, 2009), p. 3.

2. Daniel Tichenor, *Dividing Lines: The Politics of Immigration Control in America* (Princeton University Press, 2002).

3. Walter Isaacson, *Einstein: His Life and Universe* (New York: Simon and Schuster, 2007).

4. Richard Florida, *The Rise of the Creative Class* (New York: Basic Books, 2002).

5. Marshall Fitz and Angela Kelley, "Principles for Immigration Reform" (Washington: Center for American Progress, December 2009).

6. James Gimpel and James Edwards Jr., *The Congressional Politics of Immigration Reform* (Boston: Allyn and Bacon, 1999).

7. Richard Herman and Robert Smith, *Immigrant, Inc.: Why Immigrant Entrepreneurs Are Driving the New Economy and How They Will Save the American Worker* (Hoboken, N.J.: John Wiley & Sons, 2010).

8. Darrell M. West, *Biotechnology Policy across National Boundaries* (New York: Palgrave/Macmillan, 2007).

9. Michael Arndt, "Ben Franklin, Where Are You?" *Business Week*, January 4, 2010, p. 29.

10. Organization for Economic Cooperation and Development (OECD), *Science and Technology Statistical Compendium, 2004* (Paris).

11. National Science Board, "Science and Engineering Indictors, 2004" (Washington: National Science Foundation, 2004), p. 0-4.

12. OECD, *Science and Technology Statistical Compendium, 2004.*

13. Moira Herbst, "Geniuses at the Gate," *Business Week*, June 8, 2009, p. 14.

14. Lisa Lerer, "Invest $500,000, Score a U.S. Visa," CNNMoney.com (http://money.cnn.com).

15. Douglas MacMillan, "Give Me Your Smart, Your Motivated. . .", *Business Week*, March 22 and 29, 2010, p. 27.

16. Moira Herbst, "Still Wanted: Foreign Talent—And Visas," *Business Week,* December 21, 2009, p. 76.

17. Citizenship and Immigration Canada, "Analysis of Program Activities by Strategic Outcome, 2008–2009" (Ottawa: undated).

18. Darren Carlson, "Huddled Masses Welcome in Canada" (Washington: Gallup Poll, June 21, 2005).

19. *Business Week*, "Taking Aim at Outsourcers on U.S. Soil," June 15, 2009, p. 10.

20. Matt Richtel, "Tech Recruiting Clashes with Immigration Rules," *New York Times,* April 11, 2009.

21. *Ethiopian Review,* "Bloomberg on Immigration Policy," January 4, 2010.

22. Vivek Wadhwa, "America's New Immigrant Entrepreneurs," Undated paper (University of California, Berkeley, Master of Engineering Management Program).

23. William Galston, Noah Pickus, and Peter Skerry, "Breaking the Immigration Stalemate: From Deep Disagreement to Constructive Proposals" (Brookings and Kenan Institute for Ethics at Duke University, 2009), p. 4.

24. Geoffrey Sayre-McCord, ed., *Crime and Family* (Temple University Press, 2007); Michael Wadsworth, *Roots of Delinquency: Infancy, Adolescence, and Crime* (New York: Barnes and Noble Books, 1979), p. 115.

25. Galston, Pickus, and Skerry, "Breaking the Immigration Stalemate," pp. 12–14, 23–24.

26. Fitz and Kelley, "Principles for Immigration Reform."

27. Lymari Morales, "Americans Return to Tougher Immigration Stance" (Washington: Gallup Poll, August 5, 2009) (www.gallup.com).

28. Eduardo Porter, "Illegal Immigrants Are Bolstering Social Security with Billions," *New York Times,* April 5, 2005, p. A1.

29. Tamar Jacoby, "Immigrant Nation," *Foreign Affairs* (November/ December 2006): 50–66.

30. Fitz and Kelley, "Principles for Immigration Reform."

31. Pew Research Center for the People and the Press, "Trends in Political Values and Core Attitudes: 1987–2009" (Washington: May 21, 2009), p. 65.

32. Spencer Hsu, "Task Force to Recommend Overhaul of U.S. Immigration System," *Washington Post,* July 8, 2009.

33. Galston, Pickus, and Skerry, "Breaking the Immigration Stalemate."

34. Fitz and Kelley, "Principles for Immigration Reform," p. 26.

35. Russell Wheeler, "Seeking Fair and Effective Administration of Immigration Laws," Policy Report (Brookings, July, 2009).

36. Executive Office for Immigration Review, "EOIR's Improvement Measures–Update" (U.S. Department of Justice, June 5, 2009).

37. Spencer Hsu, "U.S. to Expand Immigration Checks to All Local Jails," *Washington Post,* May 19, 2009.

38. Private briefing by Marc Rapp of U.S. Immigration and Customs Enforcement, Brookings, March 11, 2010.

39. E. J. Dionne Jr., "Democracy in the Age of New Media: A Report on the Media and the Immigration Debate" (Brookings, 2008).

40. Doris Meissner, testimony before Senate Committee on the Judiciary, Subcommittee on Immigration, Border Security and Citizenship, April 30, 2009.

41. Carnegie Corporation, "The House We All Live In: A Report on Immigrant Civic Integration" (New York: 2003); Institute for Local Government, "A Local Official's Guide to Immigrant Civic Engagement" (Sacramento: 2008).

42. AILA InfoNet, "President Obama's Fiscal 2010 Budget" (Washington: American Immigration Lawyers Association, May 7, 2009).

43. Randy Capps, Michael Fix, Margie McHugh, and Serena Yi-Ying Lin, "Taking Limited English Proficient Adults into Account in the Federal Adult Education Funding Formula" (Washington: Migration Policy Institute, June 2009).

44. Michael Bloomberg Campaign Flyer, "Immigrants: The Lifeblood of New York City" (New York: Fall 2009).

45. James Tucker, "The ESL Logjam: Waiting Times for Adults ESL Classes and the Impact on English Learners" (Los Angeles: National Association of Latino Elected and Appointed Officials Education Fund, September 2006).

46. Public Policy Institute of California, "Learning English in California," Research Brief Issue 116 (San Francisco, April 2007).

47. Christopher Connell, "Empty Promises: The Unmet Need for English Instruction across Illinois" (Chicago: Illinois Coalition for Immigrant and Refugee Rights, undated).

48. Daniel Gonzalez, "English Classes for Immigrants Fall Short of Demand," *Arizona Republic*, August 18, 2007.

49. U.S. Government Accountability Office, "English Language Learning: Diverse Federal and State Efforts to Support Adult English Language Learning Could Benefit from More Coordination," GAO-09-575 (July 2009).

50. Darrell M. West, *Digital Government: Technology and Public Sector Performance* (Princeton University Press, 2005).

51. Galston, Pickus, and Skerry, "Breaking the Immigration Stalemate."

INDEX

current media environment, 82; current views on immigration, xi, 39, 89, 93–95, 98, 100–02; data sources, xiv; differences in views on immigration among ethnic groups, 98; economic conditions and, 13, 147–48; enforcement of immigration laws, xi, 103, 124–25; fears and prejudices, xvi, 1, 26–27, 42, 58, 87, 93, 95–96; goals of immigration policy reform, 2–3, 40, 128–29; historical concerns about immigrants and immigration, ix–x, 27, 87, 88, 96–97; immigrant access to social services, 89, 103–04; immigrant country of origin, 89, 100; international comparison, 5; labor market outcomes of immigration, 1, 9, 12–13, 39; levels of immigration, 96–98, 137–38; media influence, 83–84; mistrust of government, 105–06; as obstacle to effective immigration policy, 8; pathways to citizenship for illegal immigrants, 89, 104–05, 138–39; political power of public anger and anxiety, 87–88, 89–95; political salience of immigration views, 102; preference for national immigration law, 57; ranking of immigration among nation's problems, 100–02; risk of terrorism, 39; sociocultural aspects of immigration, x, 2, 4, 17–20, 39, 94; suburban immigrant population, 8; volatility, 105. *See also* Media coverage

Race/ethnicity: differences in views on immigration among ethnic groups, 98; Hispanic American political power, 58–59; immigration restrictions based on, 27, 28, 45–47, 74, 127; outcomes of immigration policy based on

family unification, 31, 32, 35; perception of immigrant sociocultural contributions, 18; recent media coverage of immigration issues, 66, 67–68; in Reconstruction period politics, 91; Second World War immigration policies, 28–29; source of public opposition to immigration, 95–96; threats and violence against Hispanic population, 114–15

Reform of immigration policy: border security needs for, 139–40; Bush (G. W.) administration efforts, 50–54; definition of relatives eligible for immigration, 136–38; goals, 127–29; implementation issues, 110; interest group willingness to compromise, 59–60; media coverage as obstacle to, xiii–xiv, xv–xvi; obstacles to, xii–xiii, 41–43, 128; prospects for Obama administration, 54–57, 59–60; public opinion as obstacle to, xvi, 8, 105–06; public perception goals, 2–3, 40, 128–29; quality of discourse on, xii–xiii, 41, 44–45; rationale, xi–xii, 24, 152–53; recommendation for independent commission to address, 62–64, 128, 146–47; unintended consequences, 153–54

Reid, Harry, 56

Religious affiliation: historical antagonism to immigrants based on, 74; immigration restrictions based on, 26–27

Remittances, 5

Research and development spending, 129–30

Ripley, William, 72

Roosevelt (F. D.) administration, x, 29

Savage, Michael, 82

Saxenian, A., 15